FOUCAULT:
AN INTRODUCTION

FOUCAULT:
AN INTRODUCTION

Hinrich Fink-Eitel

Translated from the German
by Edward Dixon

Pennbridge Books
Philadelphia

Pennbridge Books, March 1992
Translation copyright ©1992 by Pennbridge Communications Inc.

All rights reserved under International and Pan-American Copyright
Conventions. Published in the U.S. by Pennbridge Communications Inc.
Originally published in Germany as Foucault zur Einführung by Junius
Verlag GmbH (Hamburg).
Copyright 1988

Library of Congress Catalog Card Number
92-60242

Design and Typesetting: Falco & Falco Incorporated
Printing: Versapress

Manufactured in the United States
ISBN 1-880055-02-3

CONTENTS

Editor's Note: When a work has been translated into English the English title is used. Otherwise the title will appear in German, French etc.

The Publisher would like to thank Patricia Manton, James Buckwalter and Gordon Yee for their assistance in the preparation of this English edition.

THE TOTALITY OF
FOUCAULT'S PHILOSOPHY

Michel Foucault (1926-1984) is probably the most discussed philosopher in the provinces of "poststructuralism" and "postmodernism." A bibliography, which appeared before his death, listed 729 titles.[1] However, it is still not clear if he really belongs with the representatives of the intellectual currents labelled poststructuralism and postmodernism. One thing is certain though: Foucault paved the way for these intellectual movements and contributed to their continued development. Toward the end it may be said that he surpassed both movements or found a way to circumvent them.

The focus of Foucault's investigation is "power." It is his conviction that power is the principle of development and integration within our society. If this assertion is accepted as a general rule, then power as a practical principle must also apply as a principle for a theoretical system of knowledge. In fact, power and knowledge are the main themes of Foucault's work. He draws a relationship between the two and identifies them together as objects of a fundamental principle of the will. Foucault's philosophical equation of a will to knowledge with a will to power is a fundamental Nietzschean principle. At its very foundation his philosophy is a practical philosophy that combines theory and practice into one practical principle: the will.

Foucault's premature death left behind only the skeleton of a philosophy which, as in his book *The Will to Knowledge*, critically opposed [aspects of] our present age. This framework equated power with knowledge and ignited a "discursive explosion," which simultaneously became discourse's objective to control.[2]

One of the effective strategies of power consists in explaining the contents of a discourse as a secret and assigning "discourse" the task of revealing its meaning.[3] As an incoherent framework Foucault's work conceals many secrets which challenge our capacity for interpretation. Of all philosophies, no other contemporary theory has ignited the sparks of such a discursive controversy and no other system of thought has better succeeded in capturing our age and our understanding of humanity. This present inquiry intends to follow the same path and development of Foucault's important insights.

Rejecting the "poststructural" or "postmodern" philosophy of Derrida, Deleuze or Lyotard or the "macroscopic" cultural criticism of Baudrillard, Foucault was constantly a social theoretician and historian who was concerned with a microview of concrete problems in our social, historical, political and cultural reality—one of his collected writings is entitled *The Microphysics of Power*. However, the social theoretician and historian was and remained, simultaneously, a philosopher. Foucault believed that the large question he posed regarding the meaning of human existence "today" could be answered only within the context of humanity's understanding of the past. Foucault distinguishes himself from other poststructural and postmodern philosophers in that his philosophy is a social and cultural history. Jürgen Habermas called it a "transcendental historicism."[4]

The changing order of knowledge and power is historically conditioned and our ignorance of these conditions leads us to believe that our present state of existence is the epitome of humanity. Historical-philosophical reflection upon the forgotten past reveals that the anthropological generalizations that arise in the course of our daily lives are illusions. This process is achieved when reflection is able to relativize opposing opinions about humanity from different times and at different places. Foucault outlined the entire problem of dealing with our perception of the human subject within historically conditioned boundaries of power and knowledge. The theoretical disciplines that reflection incorporates are *genealogy*—the theory of power practices—and *archaeology*—the theory of discourse and knowledge. There now remains the question concerning the relationship between the two.

Because Foucault's philosophy was never finished, the task of finding a conclusive answer is left to posterity. It is not only for this reason that his philosophy appears confusing to the person approaching Foucault for the first time.

In *The Archaeology of Knowledge* (1969) Foucault has a fictitious critic of his philosophy put forth the following question:

> Are you prepared to maintain again that you have not been what people have reproached you for being? You are already preparing a way out that in your next book will allow you to emerge in another spot and to mock us as you do now with: "No, no, I am not there where you suppose me to be, but rather I am standing here from where I am able to look at you laughing."[5]

> "Yes, do you think," answers Foucault, "that writing would be that much fun for me, if I didn't prepare with a feverish hand a labyrinth in which I wandered around... One ought not to ask me who I am nor say to me that I should remain the same; this standard is a personal morality that controls the written word. We should be released from this morality when we write."[6]

Indeed, Foucault's work is a confusing labyrinth in which the author wants to be "no one" and in truth is never what he initially appears to be, that is, wandering around and subject to constant change. One could conclude that Foucault's work is a labyrinth in a temporal respect and subject to constant change.

One could also conclude that Foucault's several books are not works of the same author, but rather of many authors. If it is really true that the author doesn't know who he is or only pretends to know who he is and where he is, than how should the poor reader proceed?

Foucault had constantly formulated research projects and programs, which he never completed, but rather replaced with new projects, which likewise remained unfinished; he also carried out research projects which were never planned. It was not only because of Foucault's diffuse work methods that the development of his philosophy remained an enigma and—for many philosophers—one to avoid. Others (including the author of this book) recognize in Foucault's methods his great achievement. Admittedly, to raise Foucault's work methods to a standard procedure would have devastating consequences. Understanding his work demands the level of intellectual sensibility and discipline that Foucault himself possessed. By observing Foucault's overwhelming desire for work, which was both experimental and spontaneous, an interpretation of his work demands nothing less than an unusual degree of expertise and methodological discipline.

If Freud's statement on narcissism as the *ultra* force supporting thought has any connection to philosophy,[7] then Foucault's philosophy is a prime example of a type of non-narcissistic thinking, because it does not focus on the person [of the author] or his prejudices and values. His insights are not the thoughts of an author eager for praise and honor; they originate from a clash with reality, which his ideas confront even at the cost of incurring several contradictions. In 1984 Foucault said in the Introduction to *The Use of Pleasure* that the motive behind his work was curiosity

> the kind that allows us to free ourselves from ourselves. . . is not the critical work of thinking that which reflects upon itself? And instead of simply justifying what one already knows, what would happen if it should succumb to the arduous task of endeavoring to know how it becomes possible to think differently? It is always

absurd in philosophical discourse to prescribe to others from above
where the truth lies . . . but it has the right to investigate what
in its own thinking can be changed by attempting to think in a
way that is alien to itself. The "attempt" is the living center of
philosophy insofar as philosophy is still that which it once was,
namely an asceticism, an exercise of critical self-reflection."[8]

This quote completely expresses Foucault because it contains
all the *motifs* of his thought. However, there persists the prevail-
ing bias that great thinkers are capable of thinking only one important thought. From Foucault one can learn that the opposite
is true; that is, that thinkers are great when they allow themselves
to become agitated through a multiplicity of different things that
are directly opposed to their basic philosophy. "One should not
ask me who I am," but rather reflect upon what I say. One should
not concentrate on the "particular" or on the "self," but rather
let them be questioned by the strange and different. Perception
and thinking do not succeed simply as function, which appropri-
ates knowledge for the purpose of becoming an authoritative
know-it-all, but rather as functions that liberate the self from the
self. In short, these are functions of a self-critical alternative thinking that place the self at risk.

What is being addressed here is not only the form but the
content of Foucault's work. The liberation of the self from the
self or the disintegration of the "self" is the postmodern side of
cognitive subjectivity and the autonomy of its actions play a decisive role in the theory formation of modern philosophy.[9] In 1966
Foucault had already announced in *The Order of Things* his program for subverting modern subject-oriented philosophy by plac-
ing thinking "in a vacuum where human life vanishes."[10] To clarify
the exact meaning of "post," I will introduce Foucault not as a
postmodernist, but rather as a poststructuralist. It seems to me
that the designation of postmodernist would be too much of a
generalization and consequently would not do justice to the complexity of his work.

One of the intentions of this work is to be an introduction.

An additional intention is to treat Foucault's own statements seriously. If it is true that his philosophy constantly changed, then it is appropriate to represent it only in the context of his total development and as a continually fermenting and growing work in progress.[11] There exists the danger that an all–too–compressed and easily understandable "introduction" is impossible. The third intention is the most important: How to proceed?

"Hermeneutics" is the theory of understanding that proceeds from the principle that the details of a text can only be understood in relationship to the text's entirety and only in the context of its entire tradition. Since the understanding of the text's entirety is in turn dependent upon an understanding of its details, the process of understanding finds itself moving in a circular and spiral direction—that is, from the particular to the universal and back to the particular and so on. This process will be used here by the reader, and in order to make it easier the introduction will employ the hermeneutic method of proceeding from Foucault's entire philosophy just as the author himself finally did. In this way, a thematic unifying thread will be found that will aid interpretation and help connect the various chapters. It is my intention to depict Foucault's philosophy as it was understood in the final stages.

Underlying the entirety of his philosophy are the concepts of history, power, knowledge and subjectivity. In view of the introduction to *The Use of Pleasure*, which is the second volume of *The History of Sexuality*, we may be more precise by supplementing these concepts with an additional basic idea. The topic of sexuality is treated as a "particularly historical experience." The "three axes" or the determining factors of this experience are namely "the formulation of knowledge, which is referential, the power system, which restricts the sphere of activity, and the forms, in which the individuals can recognize themselves as subjects of sexuality."[12]

With respect to the first two points regarding the "analysis of the discourse practices" through which knowledge is formed[13] (see Chapter 2 of this work) and "the analysis of the power relationships"[14] (see Chapter 3), the "earlier works on medicine, psychiatry, punishment and disciplinary practices laid the necessary foundation."[15] Foucault alluded here to *The Birth of the Clinic* (1963), *Madness and Civilization* (1961) and *Discipline and Punish* (1975). The third point concerning the analysis of subjectivity was not treated until the second and third volume of *The History of Sexuality* (1984; see Chapter 4).

So much for the totality of his philosophy. At the beginning there occurred a "theoretical shift" that caused him to "inquire about the discourse practices that express knowledge."[16] We must consequently proceed from the first phase, whose method of analyzing problems later underwent an alteration in the second phase. At the center of the first phase is *Madness and Civilization* as well as the preliminary work to this book, which according to Foucault, contained the three axes "in a somewhat confused manner."[17] The theoretical shift to the "axis of truth" or of knowledge is at the center of the second phase. Foucault mentions here *The Birth of the Clinic* (1963) and *The Order of Things* (1966). Because he completely revised the theory of knowledge contained in these books in *The Archaeology of Knowledge* (1969) and for the first time formulated here the discourse practices as a theory, I will describe this phase in connection with this work (Chapter 2). This phase will be contrasted with the first phase containing the works *Madness and Civilization* and *The Order of Things* (Chapter 1). This is the only modification that I plan with respect to the sequence of Foucault's own development. I want to show at this juncture that the two above-mentioned books are related to each other as complementary opposites that undergo a process of sublimation in *The Archaeology of Knowledge*.

"Thanks to a further theoretical shift"[18] there arose the "axis of power" in the third phase. Foucault lists here his *Discipline and Punish*,[19] in which he describes a history of modern disciplinary and penal practices. I am adding also *The Will to Knowledge* (1976), which is the first volume of *The History of Sexuality*. In this book Foucault developed his theory of power practices (Chapter 3).

A "third shift"[20] led ultimately to a fourth phase. In the second and third volumes of *The History of Sexuality*, entitled *The Use of Pleasure* and *The Care of the Self*, Foucault had worked out in the end the "ethical axis"[21] or the axis of subjectivity (Chapter 4). So much for the "work in progress."

The subject of "sexuality as a particularly historical experience" and its three axes of *knowledge, power*, and *subjectivity* characterizes the areas of research in Foucault's philosophy. Corresponding to these are three areas of theoretical investigation: paired with knowledge is archaeology, with power is genealogy and with subjectivity is ethics. Archaeology, genealogy and ethics are, according to Foucault, historical disciplines; the last one in particular visibly belongs to the domain of philosophy. Philosophically speaking, Foucault identified all three as problematic concepts. He is concerned with

> analyzing behavior and not ideas nor societies and their "ideologies," but rather with the practices that affect the problematic conditions in which existence is and must be conceivably subsumed. The archaeological dimension of the analysis refers to the forms of problematization itself; the genealogical dimension refers to the formation of the problematization that arises from the practices and their changes.[22]

From this perspective Foucault is finally looking back upon his entire work to *Madness and Civilization* (first phase), which includes the "problematic nature of insanity and of illness based upon social and medical practices, which also define a 'normalization' process." He is also looking back to *The Order of Things* (second phase), which consists of the "problematic nature of life, language and work associated with the methods of discourse that obey definite epistemological rules." And finally he is looking back to *Discipline and Punish* (third phase) that is related to the "problematic nature of crime and criminal behavior as determined sexual activities and pleasures within the context of self-practices became problematized, which followed the criterion for an 'aesthetics of existence'."[24] If from the point of view of "postmodern" times the first three work projects have as their area of interest "the modern" then the last project is concerned with the "premodern."

The following graph has been outlined to give a better overview of Foucault's philosophy:

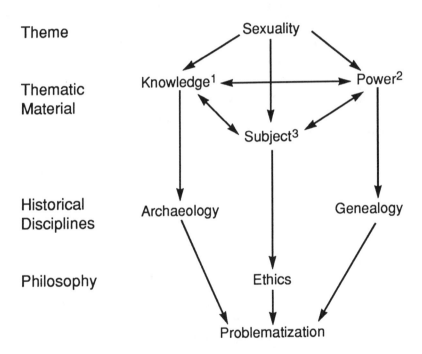

Theme	Sexuality
Thematic Material	Knowledge[1] ← → Power[2]
	Subject[3]
Historical Disciplines	Archaeology Genealogy
Philosophy	Ethics
	Problematization

Works: 1: (Madness and Civilization), Birth of the Clinic, Order of Things, Archaeology of Knowledge, History of Sexuality
       2: (Madness and Civilization), Discipline and Punish, History of Sexuality
       3: (Madness and Civilization), The Uses of Pleasure, The Care of the Self

At this point the questions that have arisen as a result of this graph must be categorized. How does the question of sexuality, for example, become part of the thematic investigation that Foucault promises to solve in his problematic analysis? What is the inferred meaning of this question for his work before *The History of Sexuality*? How did it come about that the procedures for developing the theme were arrived at before the subject itself? How and why did three changes take place for the concepts of knowledge, power and subjectivity? What is the initial reaction to the assertion that Foucault was basically concerned with power, which apparently is only one of the three procedures or axes of his main subject? Does Foucault finally succeed in integrating the three separate disciplines of archaeology, genealogy and ethics into a unified area of philosophical concern?

With a retrospective and summarized outline of his entire philosophical system we have acquired indeed a complex but also unified introduction in our interpretation process. What is the basic assumption? The "starting point" is not "that everything is evil but rather that everything is dangerous. . . If everything is dangerous, then we will constantly be busy. For this reason my position does not lead to apathy, but rather to a hyper and pessimistic activism. I believe that the ethical and political choices that we confront everyday consist in locating the main danger."[25]

Discovering the main danger in order to combat it appears to be the main motive behind Foucault's philosophy. If I have characterized the special position of his philosophy within the post-structural movement as a result of the constant position it takes on the concrete problems of our social and political reality, then a further question arises, namely what means does his theory provide for political practice to overcome the dangers diagnosed through his theory? I will pursue this question in the last chapter; however, one may say now that his theory of political action by social penal practices that follow a 'disciplinary' model."[23] In the last two volumes of *The History of Sexuality* (fourth phase) he wanted finally to show "how in the period of antiquity those becomes part of the diagnostic process only when the main danger has actually been determined.

We have now gained a further aid for our theoretical and interpretive purposes, namely the question: what are the main dangers that make up the concerns in each of the individual phases?[26] The last intention of this essay coincides with the possibility that within the discussion of danger both subject and object are identical. If Foucault diagnoses a threatening danger, then he himself becomes one as presumed instigator and profiteer of the danger. Secondly, the view that everything is dangerous and consequently endangered must be viewed in connection with his own theory. The questions must be posed with respect to those dangers that are his own. How does the uncovering of these dangers become the possible impetus contributing to their development? By assessing Foucault's philosophy from this perspective, we must formulate an interpretation of Foucault's critical theory, which is capable of critically judging not only the object but also itself. Thirdly, it must be asked wherein lie the dangers of my own interpretation? The answer to this may lie in the contradiction which the interpretation has eluded but also apparently created. Initially I have introduced Foucault's philosophy as an intricate labyrinth; as an anonymous, diverse, alterable and inchoate experimental process and open theory. I also maintain that one can adequately understand his philosophy only as a heterogeneous theory in a state of constant flux and development and not as a closed, unified and integrated system. Meanwhile his philosophy has apparently become exactly just that: a system. To accept Foucault's final thoughts on his philosophy as a complete system would run the danger of including only those aspects that fit into the system and ignoring others. Furthermore, a systematic approach would threaten the experimental openness of a philosophy whose unusual voluminosity resists systematizing.

The need for self-criticism also necessitates a critical confrontation with other views. The systematic approach to his philosophy becomes corrected in light of its inconsistent development and

vice versa. Neither side categorically denies the other, but both
depict the extremes in an incongruous situation, which under-
lies the essence of Foucault's philosophy. On the other hand there
exists the strict French rationalism of Cartesian "methods" with
its demand for analytical austerity and systematic cohesion. The
opposite side of this is an intellectual sensibility and sensitivity,
which is subsumed by the diversity of his philosophic thought.
This incongruous situation is the productive force as well as the
danger in Foucault's philosophy. It may also be of help to be more
specific with names that Foucault cited as his teachers in an interview with Paolo Caruso in 1969. The friction between them
leads to a "conflict difficult to solve." On the rationalistic side there
were "certain positive studies like those of Dumezil and Levi-
Strauss." With respect to the sensitive side of "disorder" there
existed the "passion for Blanchot, Bataille."[27] Structuralism and
surrealistic poetry, positive and scientific systematology and aesthetics constitute the dissonant relationship that is the source of
our fascination with Michel Foucault's philosophy.

In brief, the final goal of this introduction is to give a
philosophic, self-critical interpretation of his thought. Given the
accomplished nature of the situation, nothing less can be expected.

1

THE OTHER AND THE SAME

MADNESS AND CIVILIZATION (1961)

Apparently the academically trained and certified psychologist Foucault, who had worked in this field for two years at the Sainte-Anne Hospital in Paris, was not initially sure whether he wanted to become a psychologist or a philosopher. It is the goal of the treatise *Maladie mentale et personnalité* (1954),[1] to separate psychology from the classroom study of science and medicine. This separation could consequently make possible the association of the psychoanalytical method with the phenomenon of mental illness. This method proceeds from the subjective experience of the patient and not from a prefabricated case study that classifies the patient within a system of seemingly objective categories. In the same year Foucault expanded this initiative and followed Ludwig Binswanger's analytical psychology of being; he described mental illness as a forced breakdown of life's original purpose to realize and fulfill itself in freedom.[2]

At the beginning Foucault was a psychologist and existential philosopher. His plan for a philosophy based upon psychoanalysis, phenomenology, existential philosophy and the analysis of being was influenced by Heidegger's philosophy of human freedom, which likewise used Binswanger's psychology for its model. The underlying principle is that man is a being who can freely, and in accordance with his own design, conduct the existence he must live.

However, Foucault, the student of Althusser,[3] was from the start a social philosopher. In *Maladie mentale et personnalité* he wanted to reveal by means of Marxist philosophy the contradictions in the class structure of capitalistic society as the cause for the absence of social freedom, which lead to the collapse of individual freedom, and which in turn can express itself in the form of mental illness. From out of the context of psychoanalysis, existentialism and Marxism originated the theory of repression. The sexuality of the human being and it's freedom to determine for itself life's purpose are suppressed in a pathogenic manner by the conditions of social supremacy. Suppression is dramatically demonstrated in the way it reacts to the results of its own activities, namely the repression of mental illness and insanity.

These concepts are further developed in the first one of Foucault's major works, *Madness and Civilization (Folie et déraison. Historie de la folie à l'âge classique,* 1961); in the second edition (1972) the subtitle appears as the full title. It is only at this point that a psychology devised along philosophical lines becomes a philosophy guided by psychological principles. It deals with nothing less than the fate of western reason as it began to unfold in the seventeenth century during the "classical period." Foucault understands insanity as the other side of reason and conversely as a process using confinement as a means to silence itself. The archaeology of modern reason is the archaeology of silencing. It is based upon the cultural generalizations in Foucault's original theory of repression.[4] The instrument of suppression is no longer a specific social structure, but rather an entire culture (from the time of the "classical period") in which the dominant rationality, philosophy and science combine together to form, through social and political practices, a single repressive complex.[5]

In the literary and visual representations of the ship of fools during the Renaissance, insanity still signified a dark reality, a trip into the unknown where death and tragedy were certain and, of course, "personal estrangement from the world" was in general associated with "tragic madness."[6] However, the Renaissance was also aware of certain differentiations beginning with the critical consciousness of Erasmus of Rotterdam, who distanced himself from the tragic consciousness and transformed insanity into an ironically dauntless symbol for the folly and futility of life's endeavors.

In the seventeenth century the distancing was finalized. Descartes's *Meditations* (1641) presents the first philosophical evidence for the complete exclusion of insanity, which is silenced by reason[7] and reduced to idle nonexistence and stupidity. Mental exclusion was now also joined with utilitarian and social forms of exclusion. Foucault is particularly interested in two important segments in the institutional history of insanity. With the founding of the Hôpital général in 1656 begins the imprisonment of the insane. In 1794 the prisoners in the institution at Bicêtre under the directorship of Philippe Pinel were freed from their outer chains without, however, being released from their inner ones.

None other than G. W. F. Hegel provided Foucault with the main testimony for the new therapeutic concept. Hegel claims to have learned from Pinel that insanity does not merely imply the lack of reason but also "inherently" contradicts the idea of the rationally sane individual. In actuality, insanity is not a disease of the mind or intellect, but rather one of the soul (or of the "heart") to which body and spirit are directly united. In the state of insanity the natural impulses of the "heart" have gained the upper hand, conflicting, therefore, with the intellectual capacity of the human being. Insanity is cured when this capacity is (re)realized and the intellect is able, simultaneously, to separate itself from body and soul and, in turn, dominate these by reason. Hegel was able to subtly combine what apparently was impossible to combine in the medical discourses of the eighteenth, and especially the nineteenth century; namely, on the one hand, the natural

and consequently blameless determinism of madness that gains
the upper hand as soon as the human being's intellectual powers
for "integration" cease, and, on the other hand, the freedom of
the yet mentally ill person to overcome for himself the alienation which was nonetheless induced by natural determinism.

At the end of the eighteenth century the view of insanity as a mental illness is based upon the observation of a disjointed dialogue
that finalized the division and caused the uncompleted words
without any definite syntax to become forgotten; it was these
words that were perhaps analogous to stammering but also the
medium through which an exchange between insanity and reason could take place. The language of psychiatry was a monologue construed by reason that dominated insanity; psychiatry
could only exist with such a silencing of insanity. I have not tried
to write the history of this language, but rather to describe the
archaeology of silence.[8]

Foucault writes an archaeology of modern reason from the
perspective of the Other, that is, from the perspective of an insanity that has been condemned to silence by reason. However,
both are in a relationship of mutual exclusion whereby the exclusionary agent is reason. At the same time reason causes the
disproportionate imbalance in the relationship; and when viewed
from the perspective of the Other, from the non-existent entity,
reason appears as the actual cause of insanity. Moreover, in the
act of destroying its Other, reason also tends towards total self-
destruction. Foucault wanted to write a "history of the other kind
of insanity."[9] Foucault based his entire undertaking upon the possible perspective that reason could be seen from the point of view
of the Other. From this extraterritorial standpoint Foucault looks
at western culture in its entirety as a repressive entity. This means, however, that insanity is an "inseparable experience" with
"archetypal origins"[10] that should never be allowed to be totally
quieted. Indeed, insanity finds expression in the literary figure
of Diderot's "Nephew Rameaus" and "in the works of Hölderlin,
Nerval, Nietzsche and Artaud. These works are forever reduci-

ble to those forms of alienation that heal because they singularly
resist the moral imprisonment that one usually equates with the
liberation of the insane as through Pinel and Tuke."[11]

In an age when insanity had been silenced it was still possible through these works to think about a language that Foucault
had thought about in *Psychology and Mental Illness* that was "liberated and retrieved from alienation and simultaneously given back
its original linguistic character."[12] They reawakened the tragic
consciousness concerning insanity that the more critical had begun to harbor in the earlier period of the Renaissance. Foucault's
archaeology succeeds "Nietzsche's great research" wherein
"historical dialectics is confronted with the permanent structure
of tragedy."[13]

Insanity is excluded via the process of reason and redisco-
vered as the goal of Nietzsche's great research; however insanity is not the only Other portrayed by western reason. Foucault
cites also the "Orient, dreams and sexuality, the blissful world
of desire."[14] If one considers western repression as a "tragic driving
force" and that according to Nietzsche, Apollo was the God of
Dreams and Dionysus was the God of Desire (whose Western origins can be traced to the Orient) one can then understand the
importance of Nietzsche for the basis of Foucault's philosophy.
Moreover, the true concept of human tragedy in his philosophy
will become clearer.

Nietzsche saw western culture as arising through the combination of Dionysian and Apollonian elements that also prevailed
in ancient Greece. Dionysus is the embodiment of frenzy and
desire that bursts open the fixed boundaries of individuality; its
artistic expression is music. Apollo, on the other hand, is the epitome of the moderate power that shapes and defines individuality and exorcises the destructive powers of Dionysus; its expres-
sive side is exemplified through the plastic arts. The effect of the
union of the two becomes for Nietzsche *The Birth of Tragedy*,
which is also the title of his early work.[15] The incompatibility of
the two extremes, which is attributed to their different natures,

is the basic theme of this work. The way to avoid this tragedy
in western culture, a tragedy which is life itself, is to partition
the Apollonian from the Dionysian and to make the Apollonian
an absolute intellectual or "Socratic" principle that is hostile to
life. This is also the main idea of *Madness and Civilization* in which
Foucault can be seen conceiving his philosophy in the spirit of
Nietzsche's *The Birth of Tragedy*.

Foucault's early research contains the embryo of his entire
future work. In place of the research on the repression of insanity (*The History of Sexuality*) Foucault later replaced it with
"Nietzsche's great research" on the repression of sexuality. In *The
Will to Knowledge* he still hoped for evidence from the Orient
for an exemplary *ars erotica*.[16] His interest in dreams formed the
basis for his passion for surrealistic art, which wanted to express
itself "like a dream" and showed that the Dionysian energy was
not yet exhausted.

The major danger, which *Madness and Civilization* claims to
address, later becomes quite clear. Foucault sees that the root
of this danger is present in western reason, which from the very
beginning as well as throughout its development, continued to
separate itself from the Other and from its source. Therefore,
everything is dangerous and the practical consequences, which
Foucault wanted to bring our attention to, are all too obvious.
Antipsychiatry owes much to Foucault;[17] it was the example that
immediately occurred to Foucault when he answered the question concerning the motivation for writing philosophy.[18]

It may be that the three axes of knowledge, power and the
subject appear throughout *Madness and Civilization* in what Foucault calls "a rather confused manner." Knowledge appears in
the form of a juridical, administrative, scientific discourse; power in the form of interning and confining practices; and finally
the subject, which is connected with Foucault's intent to write
"a history of conditions." Among these conditions it would be possible to include the type of psychology dealing with "the relationship of the self to the self."[19] This relationship of the self to the

self began as a psychological monologue conducted by reason at the point it broke off its dialogue with its insane Other.

One must, however, emphasize Foucault's own characterization of this book; he is concerned with the "problems surrounding insanity that have arisen from social and medical practices, which have prescribed a distinctive 'normalization' profile" (see Introduction). The power practices that suppress the abnormal or unusual and attempt to conform them to the normalization profile are not only the starting points of *Madness and Civilization* but also its thematic nucleus. A condition for a possible archaeology of modern reason is contingent upon a genealogy of power practices that attempt to "rationalize" reason's Other.

THE ORDER OF THINGS (1966)

Already the next book *The Birth of the Clinic (Naissance de la clinique. Une archéologie du regard médical,* 1963): second edition 1972) was totally different. The primary concern here is not the genealogical axis of power practices, but rather the archaeological axis of knowledge. *Madness and Civilization* delves into the genealogical conditions of modern psychology while this book questions the archaeological conditions of modern medicine. If Foucault had previously inquired about the differences between the periods of the Renaissance, the "classical age" and the "modern age" (based upon the French Revolution as a temporal reference point), then *The Birth of the Clinic* concentrates on the changes from the "classical period" to the "modern." According to Foucault this topic cannot be objectively discussed when one proceeds along the usual route from the bad to the better and from superstitious fantasy to rationally ordered, empirical observation. One must rather inquire about the factual and structural changes in the medical establishment. The main theory in *The Birth of the Clinic* is that changing medical conditions provided the basis for the possibility of modern medicine. Since these changes are

merely arbitrary cultural constructs, they do not differ from the
way in which knowledge was earlier organized. What has changed
is not the semantics of knowledge, but rather its syntactical structure. As before, in the case of psychology, Foucault contested
medicine's claim to objectivity. Both are "questionable" scientific disciplines that depend upon their own cultural conception of
themselves in contingent upward trends.

In the "classical age" the process of empirical perception was
completed in the so-called rational transparency of ideal "tables,"
which were capable of general classifications as in the case of
botanical models such as family, species and type. The diseases
presented themselves as formidable types whose individual materi-
alizations appeared as injurious to ideal "purity" and the general
public. The apparent transparency of this idealized and standardized perception was superseded in 1800 by the persistent view
that claimed to penetrate the invisible darkness of the body and
elicit from it its specific secrets. The search for the pure ideal of
sickness was replaced by physicality and individuality. The idea
of recognizing a sickness after physically localizing and personaliz-
ing it belongs from that time on to the basic principles of medical science.

In 1800 the anatomist Xavier Bichat outlined the principles
of medical pathology. Post-mortem examinations and dissections
permitted an unrestricted view of the entire body. In this way
the dark, internal secrets of sickness were brought to light and
death itself was able to reveal the secrets of life. There now existed the possibility of recognizing the relationship between individual functions of existence. The basis of Foucault's anthropological structure, which concerned him at great length, is the idea
that death as the cause of finality of human individuality also
makes possible a positive science for humanity. Simultaneously,
however, a tragic awareness surfaces, which becomes the starting point in *Madness and Civilization*. These ideas previously re-
sounded in Schopenhauer's fateful *principium individuationis*,
which is the cause of suffering and which Nietzsche transformed

and subliminated through the Apollonian drive.

It also becomes clear how far Foucault eventually distanced himself from his initial position. The analysis of being and the phenomonological starting point of unrestricted individuality and of the mentally ill person's conception of self is replaced by an orientation to forms of sensory perceptions and knowledge ("deep structures" of "cognitive codes")[20] that are without a subject, anonymous, and in the case of concrete observations, also unconscious. These forms arbitrarily determine what we deem healthy and sick because they are contingent upon cultural norms. These cognitive models belong to the basic assumptions of structuralism and their real influence is noticeable for the first time in *The Birth of the Clinic*. The structuralistic turning point[21] corresponds with a shift to the opposite side. In place of introspection and unrestricted subjectivity, the extreme reverse of this appears—the body as a mute, inanimate and lifeless object.

In his interview with Paolo Caruso, Foucault mentions, in conjunction with structuralism, the names of Lévi-Strauss and Dumézil. A reference here to the positivistic cognitive theories of Bachelard and Canguilhem would be unavoidable. Bachelard[22] separated the autonomous world of scientific knowledge from the realm of everyday knowledge and biases and declared an "epistemological division" between them. Not only is the synchronous or "vertical" relationship between everyday knowledge and serious science discontinuous but so also is their diachronic or "horizontal" development. Bachelard attempted to rationally reconstruct the epochal upheavals affecting these relationships and developments over long periods of time. Bachelard's pupil, Canguilhem, emphasized on the other hand the factual successive developments of the cognitive systems and the "vertical" interdisciplinary relationship of the sciences. Foucault allied himself directly with the two cognitive theoreticians and especially with Canguilhem's investigation *The Normal and the Pathological*,[23] when he underlined the dual (vertical-horizontal) discontinuity in the relationship and development of knowledge and science (or their cognitive structures). He stresses, however, the internal and multidisciplinary investigations of a shorter time period in which the cognitive structures, science and everyday knowledge, in spite of all their differences, mutually affect each other. Only with the assumption of incongruity and separateness could Foucault begin to structurally analyze the unconscious "cognitive codes." He began to comprehend them without reference to a subject and as purely internal, formal and controlled symbolic relationships that unconsciously determine the concrete meaning of subject-related knowledge.[24]

Of course, Foucault never saw himself as a structuralist. He was not concerned with eternal and invariable structures, but rather with historical changeable ones[25] which, moreover, could be comprehended not as a closed system of laws, but rather an as an ensemble of diverse and scattered elements.[26]

In *The Order of Things* (*Les mots et les choses. Une archéologie des sciences humaines*, 1966) Foucault analyzed the cognitive structures of the "classical" and "modern" periods, which he treated in their relationship to medicine in *The Birth of the Clinic*. Furthermore, he analyzed them in the general context of an "archaeology of the human sciences," which is also the subtitle of the book. He was concerned with the archaeological foundation of the modern humanities of psychology, sociology, literature and the histories of culture, ideas and science (medicine was not included). It is surprising that the last chapter—which is about fifteen percent of the entire book—is dedicated to the human sciences. The first eighty-five percent of the book develops the archaeological viewpoint from which the human sciences are later examined.

The basis of the archaeological discussion is what Foucault terms the "epistemology" of the period under observation. With this term Foucault includes the basic cognitive processes of everyday knowledge, science and philosophy. Associated with the epistemology of the Renaissance is "similarity," and with the epistemology of the classical period is "representation" and with

that of the modern is "the human being." Along with the traditional view that each successive period reveals a continuing
progress of knowledge, Foucault, following the cognitive theories
of Bachelard and Canguilhem, widens accepted opinion. The
modern development of western rationality does not represent
an uninterrupted continuum that begins with the classical period, the Renaissance, Classicism and Descartes' Enlightenment and
continues through Hegel, Heidegger and Wittgenstein. The development from one age to the next is rather intermittent and
occurs with abrupt changes. One may also analyze the origin of
our present conception of ourselves with this view. What is under discussion here is the change between the eighteenth and
nineteenth centuries during which time a totally new perspective was introduced that emphasized the "human being."

In the Renaissance, the principle of universal similitude
governed the individual's understanding of the world. Words and
symbols were intended to resemble things and designate objects.
Through the principal of analogy one believed in the possibility
of comprehending even the smallest details of being and of envi-
sioning its totality. One imagined God as the supreme being, who
was analogous to the totality of existence. This cognitive principle contains a three-part structure. Symbol and the thing designated are joined together by an intermediary force or mediating
component consisting in similarity or natural affinity.

In the transition to the classical age, the mediating third component disappeared and from the three-part structure appeared
a two-part or dual structure. The relationship of the symbol to
the thing was now traced back to a specific point in time when
the categorization of the symbols themselves was determined.
A transparent language appeared that was based upon an abstract
order of things and organized by artificial means involving tax-
onomy and grammar. Now the cognitive-theoretical foundation
outlined earlier in *The Birth of the Clinic* becomes clearer. The
symbol now completely represents the thing designated and regu-
lates the manner of representation. The dominant logic of Port-

Royal in the classical age combined representation and thinking through the concept of imagination. Representation involves the visualization of, for example, things through pictures and symbols, which bring the things before us and allow us to image them. Thinking comprises imagination and the representation of things or circumstances in our consciousness through inner pictures and images. Thinking not only reproduces the assumed natural order of things—as was the case in the Renaissance—but also recognizes the order made for it by means of its own representational powers. In place of a natural relationship between symbols and the things designated, there came about an autonomous system of symbols that, despite their artificiality, attempted to do justice to nature in their reflection of it. In place of the infinite number of ways in which similar things were interpreted, there arose a closed order of Cartesian methods that sharply divided and classified identities and differences.

Foucault clarifies the period changes with examples. Cervantes' drama *Don Quixote* symbolized the transition from the Renaissance to the classical period. The Renaissance world of universality and analogy in which the tragic figure of the knight still lives had already been shattered. The old world of the knights, which had deteriorated to fiction in the novel, failed in its attempt to rediscover itself in reality. The continued search for analogy led to dramatic confusion. Herds of animals were not armies, windmills were not giants and maids were not courtly women. Insisting on mere similarities led to a complete confusion of real identities and differences.

Foucault illustrates the transition from the classical age to the modern by an example with which he attempts to illustrate the basic problem of classical rationality. Indeed, representations are capable of representing not only objects but also themselves as cognitive principles. The notion that concepts not only designate objects but also are capable of representing themselves can best be understood by a mental experiment. When I am thinking about something I can also image the process of myself thinking about something. However, imagining a thought process is no longer a projection of the self or a representation of the self.[27] The act of such representation is capable of representing everything, but not the representing "self" or subject. Foucault outlines this basic problem at the very beginning of *The Order of Things* with his famous and brilliant interpretation of the painting "Las Meninas" (The Courtly Women) by Diego de Velazquez. In this book Foucault illustrates the problem of the human being reflecting upon his own subjective thought by transforming in his interpretation of the picture the aesthetic structures confined to a two-dimensional picture area into reflective structures of intellectualizing.

In a nutshell, Velazquez portrayed with this picture the process of painting, that is, the representation of artistic representation. In the middle, one sees the painter from behind his canvas. The Spanish royal couple that he is painting radiate in spite of their absence. Only in a small mirror in the background of the picture are they visible. All the directly illustrated figures are peering out of the picture into the eyes of the observer; they are looking at a point that does not appear in the picture, where three possible subjects could be located: the painter as representor of the subject, the royal couple as the subject of the representation and the observing subject. Velazquez can represent the act of representation as such, because he is not portraying its subject. By the same token, by representing the representation as such, he is also unable to represent its subject.

Modern epistemology has attempted this exact same task. Since Kant, the art of representation has closed its eyes to the external world and has become blind to it by attempting from the start to represent the representing subject as the basis of the representation. In place of the Enlightenment appeared a darkening of the world. Self-representation was confined to the realm of transcendentalism, upon whose formal conditions empirical reality became dependent. With the duplication of philosophy's area of interest in the transcendental, and in the empirical, which is substantiated by the former, the subject also duplicated itself. From the start, the representation closes its eyes to the external world and consequently the representing subject is confined to his or her own limited and finite reality. Instead of reflecting nature, it is reflecting only upon itself. As a finite, empirical subject it becomes at the same time a transcendental subject, that is, the infinite basis for itself. It is simultaneously the creator and the thing created, the representor and the thing represented. We have already encountered this anthropological structure in *The Birth of the Clinic*: the finite individuality of the human being is the condition for the potentiality of its own self-objectivication and self-realization.

Kant's "analysis of finite nature" paved the way for modern epistemology. "The human being is within the analysis of finitude a unique, empirical-transcendental double, because he/she is such a being, in whom one perceives the basis for every idea possible."[28] This entity is the epistemological construct of the "human being," which attempts as a finite, empirical subject to become the infinite basis for itself; in this form it became the basis for the science of the "human being" in the nineteenth century. Consequently it occupies the place of the observed observer, of the objectified subject, that is missing in Velazquez's painting.

Based on its own epistemology of representation, the classical period developed the sciences of general grammar, natural history and the economic analysis of wealth. These sciences were succeeded in the nineteenth century by philology, biology and political economics, whereby a break is made with classical epistemology. Based on the modern epistemological construct of the "human being" language, life and work became transcendental conditions making possible human self-realization. Beginning with *The Order of Things*, Foucault presented "the problematic side of life, language and work in discursive practices, which obey definite 'epistemological' rules." However, we are quite sure that the discursive practices were not under discussion even in this book.

While language, life and work appear in place of Kant's subjectivity, the possibilities for the transcendental basis and for that
which can be substantiated by it have multiplied. The sum total
of possibilities, however, remains confined to the basic structure
of the "human being" as a made creator, objectified subject and
submissive sovereign. Language, life and work are human achievements which conceivably can overtake him. This insight can have
two consequences which more or less revert back to Kant. Kant
made the empirical reality dependent upon a transcendental reality so that both represent a heterogeneous correlation; the finite
and the infinite subject are not reducible to each other. By comparison, a positivistic science can register an objective relationship as something merely imagined (reducing subjective accomplishments to the same level), while a new metaphysics can su-
persede this one by expressing the human being as a part of a
totality, and as one who has control both of him or herself and
of the whole.

The finite nature of the human being is linked to his historical nature which spans a time beginning with his birth and end-
ing with his death. This is also intertwined in an extensive threefold
historical construct: in life itself (Cuvier); in the social production
of economic values, in which the human being must assert himself or herself as a working being with needs (Ricardo, Marx); and
finally in language (Bopp), which makes possible and also limits
his ability to communicate. The unconscious, mythical contents
of linguistics have been critically unveiled by philology. Foucault
has defined the hermeneutic work of bringing to consciousness
the unconscious conditions of actual consciousness using the example of Schleiermacher, Marx, Nietzsche and Freud, all of whom
attempted to determine the secret, deep meaning beneath the
level of the phenomenon. Human existence is controlled by powers that escape human conscious control, but which the human
being, nevertheless, strives to master.

Naturally Foucault does not contest that the classical sciences
had already selected the human being as their subject. However,

the epistemological construct of the "human being," that is

> impenetrable and primeval reality, as a difficult object and sovereign subject of every possible conceived idea finds no place in it. The modern subject of a living, speaking and working individual obeying the laws of economics, philology and biology that has been given the right to recognize these by way of an inner process and by virtue of the interaction of the laws themselves . . . all these subjects, with which we are familiar and which are associated with the "human sciences," are excluded by classical thought. It was at that time not possible, that on the edge of the world a peculiar kind of being would arise, whose nature it would be to recognize nature and consequently itself as a natural being.[29]

Along with the empirical-transcendental duality, in which the "human being" has been doubled, a further *aporetische* duality can be discovered. By way of an infinite task, "cognition" attempts to assure itself of that which has not yet been thought of. However, since that which is not yet thought of is a condition of "cognition," to safeguard itself, it must constantly submit to it (Husserl, Freud). Finally, anthropological thinking takes it upon itself to imagine a return to an original state (Heidegger) which has vanished in the prehistoric darkness of archaic life, work and language. The original state should precede historical experience as its foundation and simultaneously be imbedded within it as its object. It is appropriate to bear in mind that the loss of this original state was discussed in *Madness and Civilization*.

Now Foucault has finally reached his goal, which has allowed him to deduce the "sciences humaines" from the "triangle of knowledge." These sciences do not directly discuss the human being as a living, working and speaking being, but rather as a being that finds itself in these conditions reflecting upon itself or in the process of performing these activities. Foucault imagines the "subject of the modern *episteme*" as "an open voluminous three-dimensional area:"[30] first, there is the dimension of the formalized mathematical and non-mathematical natural sciences;[31] second, there is the dimension of the model sciences consisting of biology, economics and philology or linguistics; and, finally, there is the reflective dimension of philosophy, whose *aporetische* structures are outlined. The modern humanities represent a contingent, active, uncertain and highly questionable intersecting point of the three dimensions which in no way ought to be represented symmetrically. Consequently, psychology makes use of the model of biology which works with the concepts of function and norm; sociology makes use of the economic model which works with the concepts of conflict and controls; and literature makes use of the model of linguistics which operates with the concepts of meaning and systems. Also, the models find correlations in philosophy: a biological model is found in Comte, an economic model in Marx and a linguistic model in Freud.

The impurity and instability of the humanities result from the constant danger of their intersecting and mixing with one another which expresses itself in the elevated reproaches of "psychology," "sociology" and "anthropology." The explanation for their difficulties, "their sensitivity, their uncertainty as a science, their dangerous familiarity with philosophy, their poorly defined reliance upon other areas of knowledge, their secondary and derived nature, their claim to universality rest with the complexity of the theoretical cognitive configuration in which they find themselves and with their relationship to the other dimensions they are given access to."[32]

Foucault's criticism of the dubious rationale of the humanities likewise reveals the criticism of those who claim to reveal him as the "unmasker" of "actual" reason and rationality as nonsense.[33] Foucault is criticizing the rationale of an entire era which is in no way identical with rationality "at all." Contrary to opinion, Foucault demands more rationality, not less. This is evident in his program for the subversion of modern subject-oriented philosophy that is rendered completely in the following quote:

> In our present age one can only think in a void in which the human being has vanished. This void does not result in a deficiency; it does not prescribe a space that should be filled. It is nothing

more and nothing less than the realization of a space, in which it is finally possible to think.[34]

Pioneering this new way of thinking are the "counter sciences" of psychoanalysis, ethnology and linguistics that formed on the frontiers of the old anthropological discourse. If Foucault imagines all of these as sciences of unconscious structures, which determine or limit human consciousness from outside itself and which consequently question the human consciousness' awareness of itself as the creative cognitive power, then it becomes clear that he has only the structural direction of these sciences in mind, namely, the psychoanalysis of Jacques Lacan, the ethnology of Claude Lévi-Strauss and the linguistics of Saussure, Hjelmslev or Beneveniste.

Psychoanalysis has analyzed the "forms of finite reality," which "define the possibilities for all knowledge of the human being"[35] that pertain to death, pleasure and language. It is important to remember here that *Madness and Civilization* associated irrational insanity in a tragic connection with death and also that the "blissful world of pleasure" was the subject of the "great Nietzschean investigations." Foucault's wish for a language that is non-anthropological in nature will be discussed shortly.

Ethnology is the catchword that up to now has summarized our reflections on Foucault's archaeology of the human sciences since *Madness and Civilization*, where ethnology also forms the basis of its viewpoint. Just as psychoanalysis has questioned the dominance of human self-consciousness over unconsciousness, so ethnology doubts the dominance of western culture's historicity,[36] which is Foucault's main topic. Especially considering the fact that there were other archaic or "primitive" cultures and relics that reveal the historical relativity of the, generally speaking, highly civilized western culture, ethnology finds itself confronted with strange, and above all, unintelligible and unrecorded cultures, which it attempts to approach as a disinterested observer from the outside. Ethnology is like a stranger endeavoring to understand other strangers. Foucault applies this ethnological view to his own culture. His philosophy is an "ethnology of one's own society."[37] The attitude of the disinterested observer looking inward from without and of the stranger's relationship to other strangers defines the viewpoint which he has taken since his structuralistic change in *The Birth of the Clinic*. In *Madness and Civilization* Foucault conceived this point of view in connection with a world of insanity, dreams and sexuality inhabited by the Other, which his own culture has ignored and excluded. From this world Foucault proceeds in producing a totality of culture that becomes the Other that is alien.

Perhaps one must conceive the "counter sciences" of ethnology and psychoanalysis as a unit in order to completely understand his total viewpoint. Freud once called the unconsciousness the "inner foreign country."[38] As a foreign country, it is only accessible from the outside. Since it is, however, an inner foreign country and is therefore subject to the laws of the "inner world," it requires the alien view of ethnology in order to recognize it for what it really is, that is, the unconscious legislator that controls the affairs of "inner reality." One can best illustrate Foucault's point of view with the example of the "foreign guest worker" living in the Federal Republic of Germany.

Perceiving reality from the "outside," Foucault views the unconscious laws of his own culture that pertain to those practical epistemological structures responsible for exclusion (*Madness and Civilization*) and integration (*The Order of Things*). As complimentary investigations the two books form a single entity. The two disciplines that work with cultural ethnology are genealogy and archaeology. *Madness and Civilization* is a "history of the Other, that stands inside and outside of society. He or she is excluded in order to avert internal dangers and also included in order to reduce his or her eccentricity." In contrast to this there is *The Order of Things*, which is a *"history of the Same* (du Même). This history is simultaneously disperse and related to a given civilization according to the boundaries that constitute similarities or differences."[39]

The attention given in the first book to the opposite of the insane Other becomes in the second book the basic theme, that is, the development of western rationality. Even if the Other is not thematically underscored here, the history of the Same is viewed from the perspective of the Other. The occasion for Foucault's composition of *The Order of Things* was a story by Jorge Luis Borges. In it, a Chinese encyclopedia is quoted that deals, according to western standards, with a somewhat irrational classification of the animal kingdom. This is the same perspective of the book: alienation of the typical and transformation of the Same through a confrontation with the strange that is positioned opposite to its Other.

Consequently Foucault places the *Order of Things* in the same vein as *Madness and Civilization*, wherein Foucault traces the reappearance of the ostracized Other in the literature from Diderot to Artaud. Now the author celebrates in two intellectual areas the return of an autonomous language that has no subject and has been liberated from the human order.

The one constitutes the third "counter science" of structural linguistics whereby the concept of "language" is understood to be the pure, formal and structural arrangement of the spoken word, which can only be analyzed as an unconscious process "from the outside." This is also the manner in which Levi-Strauss proceeded in his ethnology which generalized structural linguistics as a cultural science.[40]

The other area incorporates literary works such as those by Artaud and Roussel, in which conventional language is broken down as a material that is autonomous and eventful. In the case of Artaud, language is "reduced to a scream, to a tortured body, to the material quality of thought." In the case of Roussel, language recounts the "eternal recurrence of death and the puzzle of divided origins." It consequently expresses an experience that is so unendurable it can only be manifested through insanity. In an anthropocentric sense language "frees itself from the shapeless, silent and meaningless region" and becomes an event.[41] In the surrealism of Kafka, Bataille and Blanchot, this liberation reaches completion. Language becomes a radical experience of finite reality which does not exalt or mirror itself in infinity. Within the boundaries of finite experience, language can finally liberate the human being from him or herself to a state in which he or she recognizes finitude as the boundary that encloses him. Death, pleasure and language are the forms of finite reality that make human self-awareness, as outlined in psychoanalysis, possible. Literature shows how they could formerly be used as mediums of "transgression." Due to their finite and imperfect nature, they direct attention to their opposite, to that which is beyond the boundaries of human experience.

Consequently the "language of the Other" expresses itself in both forms of the recurrence. On the one side, language manifests itself as a pure formality of an unconscious, organized system of rules existing in a world beyond; on the other side, language manifests itself in its "radical intensity"[42] as an occurrence in the material world of the here and now.

What is the danger that *The Order of Things* alludes to? The question is difficult to answer in a brief discussion. Perhaps Foucault is concerned with the practical dangers connected with the powerful institutionalization of the sciences whose status as human sciences is highly doubtful (one may consider here especially psychology and sociology). Rather than show us that our society is not far from being controlled by knowledge and the disciplines that are empowered with institutional authority, Foucault would rather show us how our present society is not far removed from a definite juridical order. This is, however, not under discussion in this work.

One can say quite frankly that *The Order of Things* is Foucault's "philosophical" book. Here the history of philosophy combines with the philosophy of life or existentialism. There is less emphasis on opposition to something and more emphasis on a direction toward something. If *Madness and Civilization* dealt with the philosophy of the Other, *The Order of Things* is concerned with a philosophy of the Other's opposite, of the human being as a finite being on the verge of a breakthrough to the Other. Influenced by Kant, Heidegger and avant-garde literature, this book outlines a philosophy of the finite world. Kant's "analysis of finite reality" paved the way for him where Heidegger's interpretation of Kant stopped.[43] His concept of "transcendence" comprised the finitude of "being" as an "opening" to a circumscribed existence that is expressed in the intransitive and self-referential language of avant-garde literature as the point of escape.[44] Again, it is incorrect to either deny[45] or affirm[46] the assumption that this book is a "postmodern" denunciation of "modern" subject-oriented philosophy. Instead, it joins us directly with the attempt of subject-oriented philosophy to think of all possibilities that would lead eventually to overcoming it [the subject].

However, it appears different if one views *The Order of Things* and *Madness and Civilization* as complementary experiments. Then one may say that Foucault was concerned in *The Order of Things* with exposing an internal, and, therefore, more precise danger which he viewed in *Madness and Civilization* from the outside. Consequently, the "first shift" (mentioned in the Introduction) caused him to question "the forms of the discursive practices that express knowledge."

CHAPTER

2

THE DOMINANCE OF THE SAME AND THE ILLUSION OF AUTONOMOUS DISCOURSE

THE ARCHAEOLOGY OF KNOWLEDGE (1969)

The Archaeology of Knowledge (L'archéologie du savoir) alleges to reflect upon the methods used in the previous works, but in actuality radically criticizes them.[1] The anonymous "historical subject" is mistakenly the topic of *Madness and Civilization*, and insanity is seen as a puzzling "primeval" experience.[2] Already, in the preface to this work, an "impossible task" has been put forth[3] for which Foucault foresees the consequences. If insanity can only be "expressed" in the form *silence*, then how can one say anything about it in reality? The complete Other does not, therefore, exist.[4]

In *The Birth of the Clinic* the analysis of the Other's opposite and of the structural order of medical knowledge commits a different mistake. Through its close orientation to structuralism it moves from one extreme to the other and analyzes the historical order of knowledge as standardized integrated "codes." Likewise, The *Order of Things* wants to have us believe that there exists a monolithic "cultural totality."[5]

Furthermore, it is not completely clear how the "history of the Other" and the "history of the Same" are related to each other.

Foucault does not make this a consideration. However, upon closer observation it becomes evident that both the Other and the Same, the interior and exterior, exclusion and integration appear estranged without any reconciliation. How do the exclusion practices that are examined from the perspective of genealogy behave in regard to the archaeological structure of knowledge? Due to the sheer negative character of the exclusionary practices they cannot be comprehended internally. And conversely, how do the epistemological systems of integration that are examined from the perspective of archaeology behave in regard to social practices? Apart from this, the archaeological strata become an abstract and floating state. According to Foucault, it is situated in the middle region between the cultural codes and philosophical reflection.[6]

In *The Archaeology of Knowledge* Foucault is apparently aware for the first time of the danger in his own theory. The danger appears to consist, as previously stated, in the irrevocable separation of the interior and exterior, the Same and the Other, theory and practice. Perhaps also because the radical criticism of the first partner in this duality has led to idealizing the second over the first, this inversion has caused the classification of the typical and same as evil, and the strange and different as good. The same holds true for similar dual concepts such as reason and folly, language and silence, unity and multiplicity, systems and anarchy, meaning and nothingness. Insanity is now "actual reason" and reason is now "actual insanity." Normality is disease and disease is normality. By romanticizing the "deeper" meaning of insanity, which stands opposed to accepted culture, Foucault had decidedly cleared the confusion since the time of *The Archaeology of Knowledge.*[7] Naturally the notion of the "Other" is totally dependent upon the premise of inversion and, in particular, the inversion of the "One."

Foucault's magic word solving this problem is "discourse" or the "discursive event."[8] By making it the center of his theory instead of madness and silence or epistemology, the previously divided partners are connected to each other. The discourses them-selves become the practices. The discursive practices distinguish themselves from the non-discursive practices (technical, institu-tional, economical, social and political). However, they not only differ but are also connected in a "formative" manner.[9] The prac-tices are therefore in this respect dependent upon the discourses.[10] Dreyfus and Rabinow speak of the "illusion of the autonomous discourses,"[11] which, in my opinion, form the second phase of Foucault's philosophy. It intensified, of course, a tendency that began since the appearance of *The Birth of the Clinic*. The jux-taposition of the first phase to the second is perhaps too schematic, since the second was already rooted in the first.

Foucault now asks about the discursive relationships (*rapports discursif*) between the discursive practices that are expression-oriented (e.g., psychopathology) and the non-discursive practices that are subject or content-oriented (e.g., mental hospitals). The discursive relationships (e.g., those involving the cultural order of values into "normal" and "pathological") are the overlapping third party standing opposite the still heterogeneous, discursive and non-discursive practices which correlate to one another. However, the last two also contain within themselves a double nature. The non-discursive practices have control over their own discursive order (e.g., institutional order) and the discursive prac-tices have their own subject and their own "milieu" (e.g., hierar-chically arranged sick calls).[12]

The correlative, heterogeneous and discontinuous discursive relationships form the archaeological layer which, as Foucault wants to uncover, contains the rules according to which knowledge is transformed into science. "Knowledge" is for Fou-cault the object of discussion for the discursive practices.

Let us now consider the systematic make-up of the discur-sive theory itself according to its subject. Discourses are in some way regulated associations or formations of "expressions" (énoncé). By that Foucault means neither the proposition (the descriptive expression), nor the grammatical sentence, nor the act of speech, which can be broken down into the smallest units within a larger system (grammar, logic and the conventional rules governing the act of speaking). In contrast to this, the "expressions" should explain what is actually said as if it were a completely individualized, contingent, anonymous and limited material substance that is localized in a definite space at a definite time. In an exterior state of complete meaninglessness, expression appears to archaeology chaotically dispersed in space. That enables Foucault to first and foremost inquire about its actual conformity to rules. For a long time Foucault was convinced that meaning that could be directly experienced and proven was only illusion.[13]

Giles Deleuze adheres to his own interpretation that Foucault had transformed his earlier theme "words and things" (which is the literal translation of the original French title of *The Order of Things*) into the topics of "expressions or that which can be said or seen" in *The Archaeology of Knowledge*, whereby visible things are involved with the non-discursive practices.[14] The relationship between the two is "knowledge" and its archaeology is concerned with uncovering the conditions for verbal and visual expressions. The active, determinant form of expression affects receptive or receiving forms of visible expression in the same way that operations affect material or speaking (e.g., psychopathology) affects content (e.g., the mental asylum). Much in the same way that expression relates to the anonymous totality of language, visible substances relate to the order of the visible world.

If discourses are regulated formations of expression, they form an "archive," a system or a universal law of regularity. The sum total of given circumstances for the formation of expressions and discourses in a certain period characterizes the general formation of the historical "a priori." On the basis of this discursive theory, Foucault polemicizes the traditional approaches to recording history and philosophy. Foucault objects especially to what he comprehends in these approaches as the final bastion of structuralism, which he terms "transcendental narcissism"[15] that has squeezed reality into a theory; into a closed, timeless, static set of conditions determined unconsciously within a structured context. In contrast to this, *The Archaeology of Knowledge* is concerned with the openness, alterability and heterogeneous make-up within discursive regularity. In place of the illusion of evolutionary continuity appears the principle of discontinuity; in place of traditional unity and categories is the sporadic incidence of discursive events, which are completely independent of the typical boundaries between everyday knowledge, science and philosophy. In the same manner the discursive analysis treats the unity of a particular discipline, work or book. The contingent and external factuality of the discursive events also finally replaces the traditional principles of subjective creation, or mysterious origins and deeper meanings which can be gleaned from texts and documents. Instead of traditional documents, created by authors, that are heavy with meaning within an interpretive construct, archaeology in the strictest sense is occupied with mute and meaningless monuments which can be unearthed from below the surface of actual, experienced sensory associations. This implies a further meaning to Foucault's definition of archaeology which is an ethnology of one's own culture.

Seldom in philosophy has one experienced a process of such contraction or self-purification. With the removal of the total Other, the dialectic of the Same and the Other, of the typical and strange (within the individual realm), dissolves into pure positivism, whose historical tendency and also problematic existential nature falls victim to the earlier works. In place of philosophical starting points there occurs an "objective" recording, collecting and ordering of given facts in the context of historical experience. The archaeological archiver is the collector and organizer, an apparently disinterested observer, whose observation of the basically meaningless material remains an external process. Never before in the course of his development had Foucault distanced himself from his original subject-oriented philosophy. Now he had discarded the ballast and perfected what he had begun in *The Birth of the*

Clinic, namely, the establishment of a connection to Bachelard's, Canguilhem's, Guéroult, Althauser and Serres's histories of philosophy and history, which he enriched with the sociological-historical insights of the historian of "annals."[16]

If one were to inquire yet more closely about the standpoint that arose from a defunct dialectic and an abandoned philosophy of life, then one again becomes aware of only a peculiar suspension over an area that is undefined and cannot be located within the supposed realm of "positivism."[17] Although a further break with the tragic undertones of his earlier work is manifest in the "merry" and "propitious" side of positivism,[18] there is still at least one continuity. Even Foucault's master, Friedrich Nietzsche, saved himself from the dramatic, tragic side of his early work through a second phase that was well disposed to the Enlightenment and to positivism. At the center of this phase stands *The Gay Science.*

It remains to be said that *The Archaeology of Knowledge* is not intended as methodology for his earlier works. This assessment is confirmed by *The Order of Discourses* and *The Will to Knowledge*, the latter of which contains a methodological program, whose plans and projects could in no way be realized in the subsequent works.[19]

CHAPTER

3

THE DOMINANCE OF THE OTHER
AND THE ANALYSIS OF POWER

NIETZSCHE AND "THE ORDER OF DISCOURSES" (1971)

The above mentioned interview with Paolo Caruso from the same
year in which *The Archaeology of Knowledge* appeared summa-
rizes precisely the theoretical foundation in Foucault's philosophy.[1]
According to Foucault, he took three things from structuralism:
first, the idea of the "disappearance of the subject,"[2] because its
experience of reality is subject to the unconscious, determining
structures; second, the idea of the disintegration of "sense," which
is understood as "directly experienced meaning"[3] and whose analysis is to be replaced by the unconscious structures which express
"the formal conditions for the appearance of sense"[4]; and finally, the dissolution of the idea of "history" as an ideal "evolutionary," linear process of consciousness.[5]

  He differs, however, from structuralists in that he is not concerned primarily with the question of the structural conditions
for the appearance of sense, but rather with its interruption or
alteration. He is concerned mainly with the discontinuous, historical conditions that are directly involved in the experience of
meaning. Moreover, structuralism makes the linguistic model an
absolute and subjects the "conditions, which are not actually of
a linguistic nature," to a "language model."[6] It is clear that Foucault means here the non-discursive practices which he juxtaposes

with the discursive practices in *The Archaeology of Knowledge*. This supports more precisely the assertion that Foucault was a poststructuralist.

The theory of *The Order of Discourses* from the aforementioned inaugural lecture by Foucault at the Collège de France on December 2, 1970 (L'ordre du discourse) is that discourse or the discursive practices are not subordinate to non-discursive practices, that is, to power and desire. A similar theory was presented in *The Archaeology of Knowledge*,[7] but now the basic conditional relationships of this book have been inverted. The practices are not dependent upon the discourses (which in the *Archaeology* are still autonomous), but rather conversely upon power and desire. Foucault now accentuates the material and sensational side of the discourses or expressions already described in the *Archaeology*. It is the goal of power to control the threatening powers and dangers of discourse, "to tame and exorcise its unpredictable sensational side and to circumvent its materiality."[8] In a delicate inversion of Jacques Derrida's well-known theory that western intellect is centered on the Logos or reason, Foucault maintains that it is, to the contrary, dominated by a Logos phobia, by a "silent fear of sensational events, of the multitude of things said, of the sudden emergence of expression, above all of everything that is violent, sudden, aggressive, chaotic, dangerous, of the great and incessant rush of discourse."[9]

Out of fear power wants to tame, diminish, control and organize discourse. Foucault lists a number of practices to control discourse: exclusion, prohibition, banning of themes, ritualization of speeches, legal incapacitation of the insane, establishing boundaries between what is true and false, (or between that which at any given time has been deemed to be that or the other). One sees that Foucault has returned to the domain of *Madness and Civilization*, to the analysis of social practices and to the theories of repression contained in the book.

Further practices to control discourse involve commentaries that subject the accidental nature of discourse to the eternal cycle of repeating itself over again. This is the principle of the author who subjects discourse to the identity of a creative subject and who forcibly disciplines and places it within an intricate system of rules and institutions in which knowledge is acquired only according to definite rules. In the end, Foucault groups the practices of discourse control into four principles of his own philosophy.

1. He contrasts the principle of "creation" with the opposite principle of inversion: in place of the creative authority arise incidents that diminish and exclude discourse.

2. He contrasts the principle of evolutionary uniformity (in different time periods) with the opposite principle of discontinuity: historical events are embedded within a contingent and discontinuous "series," which simply duplicate and multiply.

3. He contrasts the principle of originality with the opposite principle of specification: in place of an inherent meaning for the world appears a system of rules that are forcibly imposed upon existence.

4. He contrasts the principle of meaning with the opposite principle of externality: in place of meaning that is imminent within discourse, there appear only the external conditions that make discourse possible.

If the first counter-principle describes the process of the *critique*, then Foucault uses the three other counter-principles in relation to the methodological concept that will guide his research in the 1970s, that is, *genealogy*. We see how Foucault associates himself and at the same time distances himself from structuralism. Critical genealogy replaces the structural premise of a timeless, invariable closed system of rules with the adoption of a variable and open "interplay" of various and contingent occurrences. The radical subduing of a unified structure to an open interplay of different, that is, heterogeneous and discontinuous relationships, is considered the characteristic of post- and neostructuralism.[10] Of course, the concept of multiplicity is considered in general the magic formula for the postmoderns.[11]

Whenever I spoke of the genealogy of repressive practices

with respect to *Madness and Civilization*, I was perhaps a bit hasty. Foucault adopted the concept and process of genealogy only at the time of his renewed debate with Nietzsche at the end of the 1960s. In his essay *Nietzsche, Genealogy, History* (1971)[12] he contrasts the metaphysical theory of Nietzsche's ideal and supersensible *Origins* with the genealogy of descent. The genealogist proceeds from a modern problematic situation which compels him to inquire about the actual origin of a historical event, and which he analyzes in its unique factuality without regard to teleological assumptions and final causes. He climbs down from the sublime Olympian mountaintop of the philosophers and replaces the "bird's perspective" of their intellectual dialogue throughout the centuries with the "frog's perspective" of the low points of real life, of the most minute chance occurrences, of the basest pettiness and unpleasantness. Under the subversive eye of the genealogist the familiar historical relationships deteriorate in a multitude of contingent areas of origin and intersecting lines of development. His object is not the production of sublime ideas but rather the body with its drives and powers. From this perspective history appears as a constant confrontation between the powers; as a sequence of power struggles, overcomings, victories, resistances and defeats. *The Birth of the Clinic* had already advanced to the subject area of physicality; however, now the body is not treated as a motionless, dead object, but rather as a living organism whose will to expression becomes a power.

Foucault especially adopts a basic assumption in Nietzsche's genealogy without which the analysis of the discourse controls that were developed in *The Order of Discourses* would not be comprehensible. If all abilities and achievements of the human being are expressions of his or her will to power, then so also are their subtlest discursive and intellectual accomplishments. The discourses are subject to the will to power which struggles with them for control. The will to knowledge is a will to power. Knowledge and science are not striven after for their intrinsic value, as postulated by the anti-Aristotelian Friedrich Nietzsche, but rather serve as a means to power, for guidance in a difficult world, for the implementation of one's own interests, for deception and evil. Because this insight and its historical-theoretical consequences are unpleasant, the human spirit is inclined to deceive itself—as Plato already did—and mislead itself with a, so to speak, disinterested will to "pure" truth, which cannot be the ambiguous assertion of a will to power of one whose rank is that of the possessor and guardian of truth! The human spirit deceives itself further when it imagines itself the sovereign subject of its cognitive and speaking activities. This is nothing more than a deception instigated by grammar. In truth its conscious cognitive activities are subordinate to the unconscious structures of a language, which means the disintegration of the subject—a tendency already present in Nietzsche.[13]

It is clear that around 1970 Foucault's thinking experiments are of a rather self-critical and searching nature. They are on the path of spotting the dangers and difficulties of his own theoretical endeavors and are looking for a new position from which to master the dangers. The beginnings of his theoretical endeavors lead to the "theorizations" in The Birth of the Clinic, The Order of Things, and The Archaeology of Knowledge which bring with them the danger of losing sight of the practical dangers that Foucault was especially concerned with exposing and combating. Consequently there occurred the second theoretical shift (see the Introduction) to the "axis" of the power practices whose analysis forms the center of Foucault's third developmental phase. In the meantime, it was May 1968 and in the same year Foucault had become the director of the philosophical department at the newly founded University of Vincennes. At this intellectual center of protest he succeeded Nietzsche as the heir to the leftist-radical criticism of culture. With a professorship for the History of Rational Systems, which he accepted at the end of 1970 at the Collège de France, Foucault wanted to continue the research he had begun at Vincennes. In the 1970s, in place of the "theoretical" archaeology of the 1960s, the "practical" genealogy of power appeared. At this point the concern was no longer with the discursive order of the Same or, as it later would be called, the organizing achievement and equalizing effects of the discursive process, but rather with the opposite non-order of the Other, of the non-discursive practices.

This formulation is inexact. Upon closer analysis there appears to be an alarming lack of clarity. The Other of the discursive order of the Same was previously insanity. This Other has, however, turned out to be a power. Its supervision is indebted to the order of discourse that replaces the insane disorder of the former Other. Conversely, discourse as the former quintessence of order for the Same now contains the anarchist disorder of dangerous uniqueness and materiality. I just said that everything has been turned upside down. The former Other is now the Same, and the former Same is now the Other. According to the methodic directions from *The Order of Discourses* criticism must function as a process of inversion. Foucault seems to have resolutely taken this process to heart in his own self-criticism. There is even a double inversion. The practices are not dependent upon the discourses but rather, conversely, the latter is dependent upon the former. And now the Other of the discourse is no longer the paragon of disorder but rather of order, just as now the Same is no longer the quintessence of Order but rather of Anarchy. What is now, however, the meaning of "power?" Apparently it implies ordering control, submission, repression, force, and indeed fear—but fear of what? Of the menacing "not exactly imaginable powers and dangers" of the "power(s) and the dangers of discourse."[14] Furthermore, discourse, which is the opposite of the repressive order and itself must be controlled, is consequently a "power." How are both "powers" related to each other? How can "power" contain two principles that exclude the Other, namely, order and anarchy? Is Foucault ambiguously using here two different concepts of "power?" Or is he providing a comprehensive concept of power?

DISCIPLINE AND PUNISH (1975)

Nietzsche's systemic version of the ethnology of culture is his *Genealogy of Morals* (1887). According to this work, the sociological effect of modern, moral norms rests upon the inner horror of the individual's conscience and consciousness of guilt. Conscience is an inner sanction. Its internalization is due to external, violent punishment and it presides over cruel self-punishment as soon as a transgression against moral norms begins to appear or transpires. The process of civilization and moralizing is based upon the bloody authority of cruel punishment, that has, so to speak, continually beaten social responsibility and liability into the consciousness of the people.[15]

Moreover, the ideal of moral blame goes back to the equivalent principle of economic debt. The injured party wants to compensate for the damage that was done to him or her with the equivalent degree of suffering to the wrongdoer. And so that this compensation has the effect of a public deterrence, the moral pretext is celebrated as a public festival of cruelty and torture.[16]

Discipline and Punish begins with a description of such ceremonial cruelty. In 1757 François Damiens was publicly executed because of an unsuccessful assassination of Louis XV. He was brutally tortured, quartered and burned. In such a way the injured integrity of the sovereign's person was restored by compensating him with the equivalent of martyrdom.

Aside from its connection to Nietzsche's *Genealogy of Morals* this book is also directly connected to *Madness and Civilization* and the discussion of the repression practices contained therein. Foucault constructs his genealogy of power in such a way now that he contrasts the exclusionary structure of power, which he portrayed at first through the example of the medieval treatment of leprosy, with another basic structure that can be understood through the example of the social and political treatment of the plague.[17]

(1) The first type of power is *exclusion*. Its crassest form is

physical annihilation as it was practiced in the witch hunts and in the absolutistic punishment rituals. Exclusion also implies abandonment. Examples of this are the banishment in the Renaissance of the insane, who were simply sent away, and the lepers in the middle ages, who were abandoned in leper colonies on the edge of town. And finally exclusion means internment or confinement, as was practiced in the "Hôpital général" or as in the case of the plague victims, who were placed under quarantine, isolated and carefully supervised and guarded. This last strategy for the implementation of power proved later to be the most effective because it did not require a massive power of organization for the exercise of absolutistic punitive measures; moreover, the exposure to danger and also to "free" asocials was eliminated. Since the model of the plague city helped to acquire a varied and discriminating knowledge of control and organization methods, it was even more efficient as a power model of internment, which *Madness and Civilization* depicts with the example of the "Hôpital général." Here the different types of asocials were diffusely mixed together. Of course, the later development of the power practices, according to Foucault, was based on the model of the plague city, of isolating and differentiating confinement practices, which indeed, as we will see, occurred in two forms.

With regards to the absolutistic punitive practices, the secrecy of the judicial proceedings corresponded with its display of public ceremony, whose purpose it was to discover truth. The accused was expected to confess his deed. If need be, a confession was forced by means of torture. The body played here a three-part role. First, it was punished by means of corporal chastisement, and its subjection to torture encouraged; secondly, the "truth" was forced to appear; finally, the truth was "proven" and given witness through the public display of the tortured. Of course, such punitive practices had a further disadvantage in addition to the one already mentioned: the observing public were sometimes inclined to side with the victim and to insurrection.

(2) The second type of power principle is the "inner confine-

ment" of normative *integration*. One can perhaps comprehend it as the transforming continuation of the most effective methods of the first power principle. It is no longer merely a concern of exclusion and confinement, but rather of a defined integration for those presently isolated. It was possible to change them through treatment or education and to reintegrate them into the social system. Economic strategies of normalization and inner disciplining appeared now in place of public authority with its extravagant demonstration of power. The restricting of external authority to given situations was now superseded through the general application of intellectual norms. We were acquainted with this model in *Madness and Civilization*. It is the model of the modern asylum that became the predecessor of the classical internment institution.

The enlightened lawmakers who were for reform criticized the cruelty and arbitrariness of punishment and demanded a humanization of sentencing. Criminal acts no longer offended the feudal sovereign who took revenge on the criminal, but rather they offended the entire democratic society that was obliged to defend itself against him or her. That which was to be addressed through reformed criminal laws was not the body, but rather the soul, which was to be influenced, changed and made to adapt to normative conditions. Punishment served simultaneously as a deterrent and means of instruction. It involved the public demonstration of morality. Foucault has now reached the actual theme of Nietzsche's genealogy of morals: morality is a tool for the inner disciplining and normalization of the human being.

Nietzsche overlooked, of course, one thing. Paralleling the noble project of a criminal law system that was based on morals were social changes which were not quite so highminded. In the modern performance-oriented society, vagrancy and thievery counted among the worst offenses against the work ethic. The police and the judicial officers were supplied with a more comprehensive and effective means of power than any of the other methods that the non-economic authorities of absolutism had at their disposal.

(3) Foucault now asks why, during the transition from the classical to the modern period in the nineteenth century, was neither the one nor the other model implemented, but rather a third, namely that of confinement and arrest? How did the "birth of the prison" happen? Why did it simply turn around the absolutistic punitive model, that is, public court proceedings with secret execution of the sentence? How did the model of clandestine, physical, enforced restraint become implemented despite the criticism of enlightened magistrates for reform, for whom punishment especially represented a public and moral affair? Why did the "compulsory, corporal, quarantining and secretive model of punishment push aside the stately, imposing, public, symbolic and collective model?"[18] In keeping with Nietzsche's thinking, it is indeed the stated intention of *Discipline and Punish* to enquire about the relationship between the "modern soul" and the modern punitive system.[19] In actuality the modern judge is as concerned with the spiritual constitution of the accused as he or she is with the committed act of the accused. He cooperates with psychologists, psychiatrists, educators and finally public officials for resocialization purposes. However, Nietzsche apparently overestimated the actual social effect of the "modern soul," of modern moral feelings and of the conscience. Foucault's real topic is the political economy of the body which, in the form of non-discursive practices of corporal disciplining (e.g. prisons), eventually predominated over moral discourse and the discursive beginnings of a legal reform system.

The new insights of Foucault's power theory translate power not only as repression in the form of exclusion but as a negative, suppressive force. Even the second type of power equally pursues a positive and productive purpose of social integration which Foucault, of course, did not immediately evaluate, and if he did, he probably did so rather negatively in keeping with Nietzsche. The third type of power is productive discipline, the political economy of the body, which is ultimately positively characterized by productivity. He continued the confinement model of the first power type in another direction: his goal is confinement, isolation, supervision and transformation of the body. Jeremy Bentham's "Panopticon" from the year 1887 is typically the ideal model that condenses disciplinary power, so to speak, to an architectural form. He depicts an institution that monitors and confines, in which the single cells are placed in concentric circles around a centrally located watchtower. All of the prisoners can be seen by a central guard, who himself remains unseen. The watchtower can remain unoccupied, since the prisoners will inevitably behave as if they were exposed to the watchful view of a constant observer. They supervise themselves.

Bentham's model should find an application not only in prisons but also in factories, schools, correction centers, poor houses, insane asylums and hospitals. Isolation, total organization and controls, complete transparency and constant supervision of self occurs in the absence of a visible controlling power center: this is the utopia of disciplinary power.

There is a history that antecedes this. In cloisters, theological colleges and barracks the rooms were divided, parceled, organized and controlled; the individual bodies were divided into individual movements, gestures, attitudes and energies, in order to be able to train them individually, organize them differently and finally to integrate them into a total body that comprised the many individual bodies. One may consider here the army, which after the invention of firepower became a strategically integrated and dynamic body of powers, or the factory with work departments for a differentiated and integrated modern body of production. The factory is also a good example for how the modern disciplinary power has not only a repressive but also a productive effect which increases the power forces.[20]

The third type of power combines the effects of power from the first and second types, namely, exclusion and transforming integration. The prisoners are not only prevented from interacting with society, separated and isolated but also subjected to disciplining measures such as compulsory labor. Techniques for the formation of the body take the place of the pastoral labors of the second type; the criteria for moral norm setting is replaced by that of normalcy. The disciplinary techniques serve the purposes of normalization.

It is one of Foucault's most provocative theories: the prison, which claims to remove the offense, is likewise responsible for producing it. It does not so much serve the purposes of resocialization as legitimizes the implementation of a more perfect supervision and repression apparatus.

Beyond that the non-discursive practices of corporal disciplining do not maintain constant contact with the discursive practices of science. The isolating and training disciplinary practices present especially to the human sciences precise knowledge about individuals. However, the sciences have also at their disposal their own disciplinary practices. In the process of testing, the production and the control of knowledge combines forces for the supervision of knowledge. Foucault now undertakes to genealogically reformulate his archaeology of the human sciences. The isolated, calculable and self-supervising disciplinary object is now the genealogical requirement for the rise of the human sciences. Their investigative and abstract synthesizing activity presupposes the analytical power effect of dissecting, isolating and individualizing. Subjectivity is a product of power insofar as subjectification is synonymous with subjugation.[21]

The disciplinary power has at the same time an analytical-isolating and also a synthetic-integrating influence. It combines exclusion and integration, power and knowledge; at the same time it also has individualizing and subjective-causing effects. In the disintegration of all former dualisms (of the Same and the Other, of repressive discourse controls and anarchic discourse multiplicity), power has a tendency consequently to become a totalitarian principle that is characterized as a principle of productive monism. In this way, Foucault eliminates ambiguity, which had plunged *The Order of Discourses* into a state of terrible confusion. Power is the one connection between integration and productive discipline that does not suppress subjectivity and individuality, but rather first and foremost produces it.

Foucault's genealogy of the prison[22] claims to uncover and combat the dangers, which even today have lost nothing of their threatening nature. Perhaps the danger of "Panoptism," of complete supervision and control, has even increased in the age of electronic data-processing (consider here the critical battle of data safety with the executive powers and also the tremendous power potential that could fall into the hands of an authoritative state or dictator). Or consider the dangers that form in the underground of a democratic society, behind the walls of institutions and in subversive circles of the secret service which are on the other side of justice[23] and which become even more effective the more secretive and invisible their non-discursive practices are able to operate. Finally, consider the danger of our very own subjectivity that is in truth the product of disciplining and normalizing powers.

THE WILL TO KNOWLEDGE (1976)

The Will to Knowledge (La Volonté de savoir) is the first volume of the research for *The History of Sexuality* (Histoire de la sexualité) that concludes Foucault's life work. The entire title for the German edition was expressly requested by Foucault. He was not concerned with a history of sexual behavior, but rather with the manner that it became an object of knowledge. He was concerned with sexuality as a historically unique experience (see Introduction). Moreover, he wanted to examine the way in which the discourse practices, through which knowledge forms, combine with the power practices. From the very beginning I characterized Foucault's entire work with these three concepts: knowledge, power and sexuality.

Discipline and Punish examined predominately the non-discursive power practices of corporal discipline. Already the title *The Will to Knowledge* suggests that the discursive, knowledge-producing practices will be the main topic. According to Deleuze's model, the first book concerns the order of visible things, for example, the architecture of internment institutions, within which the silent practices of corporal training are performed, and the latter book concentrates primarily on the order of spoken things. Both books combine to form a complementary examination of the total power-knowledge complex within which the conditions of the non-discursive visible world are combined with the discursive world of the spoken word.

Non-discursive power is a central issue in *Discipline and Punish*, but the power-knowledge complex was also a central issue in connection with the development of the humanities. For the very purpose of identifying the power-knowledge complex, Foucault introduces the concept of *mechanism*, which forms the conceptual basis in the third phase of his work.[24] If the discourses connected individual expressions according to definite rules of formation, then the mechanistic power strategies connected discourses and practices, knowledge and power. In the first phase, inner and outer, the Other and the Same, non-discursive and discursive practices stood in a complementary and symmetrical relationship (of course completely undetermined). *Madness and Civilization* examined the one while *The Order of Things* examined the other. The unsolved question was how both were actually related. The answer Foucault gave with *The Archaeology of Knowledge*, in the second phase, involved their asymmetrical assimilation into *one* predominant side, which as always is the heterogeneous totality, namely, the order of discourse. The discursive relationships *contain* the discursive and non-discursive practices.

In the third phase, on the other hand, both are asymmetrically combined predominantly on the *other* side. The *mechanism* of power *contains* the discourses and practices, knowledge and power. I spoke earlier, therefore, of a monism of power. It has already become quite clear why it is the power practices that now contain the discursive order of knowledge. The will to knowledge is itself a will to power that was already suggested in *The Order of Discourses* and follows Nietzsche. Foucault has now completely attached himself to the basic assumptions in Nietzsche's philosophy. It may now appear clearer why I initially said that "power" is Foucault's theme.

At the beginning of *The Will to Knowledge* the reverse process of the criticism Foucault designed in *The Order of Discourses* is applied. The object of the criticism is the "hypothesis of repression." Power is not primarily repression, dominance, prohibition, forbidding; in short, it is not a negative factor that presupposes a positive factor as its dual counterpart which it suppresses. Marx and Freud thought somewhat this way in their conception of class supremacy and suppression of sexuality. The Freudian-Marxist model of Wilhelm Reich or of Herbert Marcuse combines them both. This combination, which Foucault himself had espoused at the beginning[25], acquired a considerable following especially after 1968. Foucault draws now, however, the consequences from the new theory of power in *Discipline and Punish*: power is conversely a positive factor, whose productivity consists in that it has a general integrating effect that creates the social reality. In place of a creative-revolutionary subject—which in a struggle against repression attempts to liberate its sexuality and actual needs—appears, in a monistic fashion, a power that encompasses everything and no longer recognizes an external opponent.

What the *criticism* implies is cleared up more exactly by *genealogy*. Sexuality is not so much suppressed as it is at all times exposed to a compulsive need to confess guilt. It is not forbidden and hidden, but rather *conversely* dragged in all its details to the surface. In the medieval practice of confession in the Christian church the desires of the flesh were considered the source of sin. Like a "hermeneutic study of desire" the faithful were obliged to reveal their most secret sexual impulses. In the eighteenth century administrative measures dealing with population and politics aroused interest in health, nutrition, life expectancy, working potential and fertility of the population; consequently an interest for data that was styled on economy and biology increasingly drew attention to sexuality. Later it became an actual focal point of interest in pedagogical, medical and psychiatric institutions. In these institutions and in their related sciences sexuality was subjected to the ever-increasing "discursive process." Appearing historically late as a category in the nineteenth century, "sexuality" is nothing more than a product or construct of "discourse." To be more exact and in contrast to "sex" as the apparent natural act of desire, sexuality is the quintessence of an all encompassing *mechanism*. According to the definition of the concept, discourse and practice are combined within it; by virtue of a "complex and diversely active *mechanism*" one was able to "attach discourse with sex."[26] The "repression hypothesis" had *conversely* maintained that attempts were made to exclude sex from discourse.

The process of discourse now explains the main means of the will to power, which asserts itself as the will to knowledge. The cultures of India, China or Rome had an *ars erotica*. The West, on the other hand, has a *scientia sexualis* in which desire and love are replaced by a continual discussion about them. We promise ourselves happiness and liberation from the clutches of repression that stifle sexuality and don't notice that that from which we are expecting liberation and happiness is nothing more than the product of the power we are combating. And apparently natural "sex" is only an experience, so to speak, bait for the *mechanism* of "sexuality."

Foucault explains sexuality's manifold effects according to poststructural methodology as he had developed it in *The Archaeology of Knowledge* and in *The Order of Discourses*. The discursive encroachments on "sex" expand in an explosive fashion and supply power with the most multifarious points of support within the mind of the individual that is to be exposed. One must view the *mechanism* of sexuality like a net that encompasses the entire "body of society" and is made up of diverse heterogeneous points and intersecting lines which stand for the discursive and non-discursive institutional practices. Parents, educators, doctors, psychologists, psychiatrists and the "sanitary police" define and are in charge of "sexuality." The old European need for confessing guilt has reached a culminating pinnacle.

At this point Foucault reformulates the already designed genealogy of the modern humanities in *Discipline and Punish*. Only with the continual need to examine oneself, to make sure of oneself and to confess the most secret impulses of desire and pleasure has the individual been kept in constant touch with him or herself. Consequently, Foucault begins in the tradition of modern philosophical discourse which attempts to find truth within the self's transparent subjectivity. One is reminded here of Montaigne, Pascal, Rousseau or Kierkegaard, who all perpetuate the tradition of Augustinian "confession." However, the genealogical truth is that true subjectivity is to be found in power. It puts into action, first and foremost, the individual and subjective effects of hermeneutics dealing with desire which make available to the individual a strategy for achieving goals and the practical knowledge for obtaining them. Subject means the one subjected or subjugated.[27] This becomes especially clear in the "medicinal effects caused by the act of confession."[28] If the sexual is pathological or pathogenous, then the medical and psychiatric truth concerning sexuality creates a monopoly on therapy that aims at "normalization."

Let's stop for a moment. The attentive reader is probably already a little perplexed. Hadn't Foucault already spoken about the "pleasurable world of desire" in *Madness and Civilization*? Didn't he himself from 1954 to 1970 up to *The Order of Discourses* adhere to the "hypothesis of repression" inasmuch as in this lecture the repressive and exclusionary measures of the "discourse police" were under discussion, which, because they were afraid, suppress the threatening uniqueness and materiality of discourse?[29] Didn't Foucault belong consequently to those who paved the way to the revolts in 1968 which lead to a Renaissance of the critical theories of repression and especially of Freudian-Marxism?

Indeed. One must read his criticism of the repression theories as an unsparing form of self-criticism. It must be noted that Foucault did not say that the hypothesis of repression was wrong. It is rather only too simple. It overlooks the completely complex, productive and consequently somewhat more dangerous mechanisms of power. Its theoretical use is therefore rather limited and politically dangerous. While the hypothesis celebrates freedom's potential, which in actuality is a product of power from which it wants to liberate us, it finds itself still sitting in the trap. Sexuality and subjectivity are not powers that oppose the liberation from power, but rather are its composition—a vicious circle.

The third phase leads consequently to a renewed radical revision of the theory. It begins with *Discipline and Punish*. *The Order of Discourses* is a transitional text that vacillates between the earlier repressive-critical dualism and the later productive monism of power. Indeed, already here the archaeological conditions for the relationship between knowledge and power have been turned upside down. *The Order of Discourses* owes its existence to power. However, only with *Discipline and Punish* does power appear as the all-encompassing structure that produces the real social conditions.

When I spoke in the Introduction of Foucault's basic line of thought, which hit upon the condition of the age and our own understanding of self, I meant among other things that which has just been said. Foucault's attacks appear especially to concern the most loyal of readers. He appears to want to depart from the revolutionary hopes and promises of May 1968. What remains of the repression hypothesis appears as a narcissistic "gain for the speaker,"[30] who gives the impression of him or herself as the revolutionary subject involved with the liberation from repression.

Foucault explains the productive accomplishments of power which are more complex than the simple repression hypothesis could ever imagine them to be. Its four strategical complexes consolidate to the *one* all-embarrassing *mechanism* of sexuality, which includes the pedagogical influences on innocent sex, the association of hysteria with the female body, the psychiatric attention to perverse desires and the socialization of procreation behavior. The child, the woman, perverts and couples are the targets of practices that "develop a specific knowledge and power *mechanism* around sex"[31] and consequently produce at that point "sexuality."

In *Discipline and Punish* Foucault especially analyzes the "disciplines" that serve the purposes of training the individual bodies. In addition to that he now adds the "regulation of the population"[32] which, since the middle of the eighteenth century, as a result of especially political and demographic measures, had global effects on the entire "body of society." Each of the four strategies combines in its own way both techniques of disciplining the body and regulating the population. The final outcome of the mergers results in "sexuality," which is the most important "enforcement medium" in what Foucault finally calls "bio-power."[33] Bio-power appears as a "power to live," which replaces the old and sovereign power of death.

With this diagnosis Foucault's ethnology of his own culture draws to a close. According to Dreyfus and Rabinow it connects archaeology and genealogy to a kind of "interpretive analysis."[34] Genealogy is rather a hermeneutic-interpretive discipline which, from an involved point of view of urgent problems in the present age, attempts to show how the existing formation of discourse (e.g. those of the sciences dealing with sexuality) have arisen from the history of definite practices (like those of the Christian pastoral practices). Genealogy inquires about the origin of the modern subject with his desires and his need for confession and also inquires about the human sciences that have been assigned to him (or her). Archaeology, on the other hand, is rather an analytical discipline, which exposes within an "objective" context the unconscious order of discourse and knowledge whose practical origin was demonstrated by genealogy. It reveals that the basis of what was in the past and is today considered reality is in truth only a historically contingent construction or an interpretation. Consequently, for example, what we consider our most innate sexuality and subjectivity, is in truth nothing more than an arbitrary construct or power which we daily are duped by. Dreyfus and Rabinow see Foucault's special accomplishment in his joining together of the relationships of the human sciences, which Thomas Kuhn's theory of science achieved much in the same way with respect to the natural sciences. In contrast to the unambiguous status of the "normal" sciences, "the dubious, unconventional status of the human sciences consists in the fact that they are inextricably intertwined with the historical power structure."[35]

The Will to Knowledge is not only an "interpretive analysis" with respect to a subject, but rather a *metatheory*, which is a methodical reflection on the basic concept of power. Foucault now says, as he did previously (also in *Discipline and Punish*): power is no longer that which it was always believed to be, namely a sovereign control center which enforced its law by proceeding from above to below. It is not a possession and not merely a degree of power; it is not an ability or a means that allows one to accomplish a particular goal. Power is the war of all against one another, the total complex of eventful and momentary confrontations between bodies; the complex, decentralized network of individual, local and antagonistic power relationships. From these relationships there can also develop in a direction from bottom to top global power strategies or entire *mechanisms* (for example the state). Resistance belongs to a power relationship that is an "opponent" to power, an opposing power, which can spread out to a global strategy (for example, a revolution). Power is everything. Foucault's theory is a monism of power based on an infinite, open pluralism of local, unequal and unstable power relationships.

Let's take for example the *mechanisms* of sexuality. The power relationships between the child on the one hand and parents, teachers and doctors are intertwined with those that group around the woman (as mother), the pervert (which, it was feared, the child could develop into) and the couple (the parents as the social "basic unit" of healthy and controlled procreation). These four power fields group continually around the two power centers of discipline and of control; for example, in the school, in psychiatric treatment, in the Public Health Office, which adopt precautionary measures against AIDS, in juvenile courts, where adolescents are held responsible for their perversions, and finally in army barracks, where individuals are straightened out. The disciplines and the controls join together to form a functional complex for bio-power (which in the case of AIDS coordinates the political, sanitary, scientific, pedagogical, judicial and policing measures without the existence of a central authority to regulate the multiplicity of regulations).

Bio-power: do not forget that the will to power for Nietzsche was the quintessence of life.[36] In *The Will to Knowledge* power is considered a unity, which comprises a heterogeneous multiplicity of power relationships. This is exactly the structure of Nietzsche's later metaphysics for the will to power.[37] Foucault is (sometimes meant ironically) Nietzsche's double. His work repeats Nietzsche's philosophy under the influence of French conditions in our century. At the very beginning it proceeded from Nietzsche's early pessimistic work, from the philosophies of Dionysus and Apollo, which are united in *The Birth of Tragedy*. In *The Order of Things* Foucault reshaped the theme of the human being's finite nature into that of his or her end (or death) and in so doing oriented himself toward Nietzsche's dictum of God's death. This at the same time evoked the death of humanity whereby the world has not lost its center of meaning. The death of humanity means here the radical decentralization of the post-theological and anthropocentric picture of the world. Thereupon Foucault repeated Nietzsche's enlightened and positivistic phase and turned to his genealogy of modern power relationships. As we have seen, he became the successor and heir to the older Nietzsche by adopting from him the metaphysics of the will to power.

Why, however, does an analysis of sexuality (and not, for example, of economics, politics or law) promise Foucault an answer to the question of modern power? I see two opposite basic motives at work, one earlier and the other later. The one concerns sexuality as the Other of the dominant culture which, through exclusion, becomes known as such. The other motive concerns sexuality as the quintessence of the dominant culture, whose ethnology Foucault undertook to describe as an apparent contradiction.

Nietzsche is first and foremost the father of these thoughts. From his teacher Schopenhauer, who anticipated the work of Freud, Nietzsche had learned that the sexuality of a human being reaches into every aspect of the intellect[38] so that it represents something of an anthropological principle. In *The Birth of Tragedy* sexual desire belongs to the Dionysian side whose eruptive power threatens to overthrow the accomplishments of the perfectly shaped surface of Apollonian culture. The "Dionysian world of desire" alongside dreams and insanity was for Foucault in *Madness and Civilization* the Other of the all-too-Apollonian culture of the West which is solely rationalistic and separated from the Dionysian. Already at that time Foucault had in mind to undertake an analysis of sexuality which was intended to resume one of the "great Nietzschean investigations." If one wants to understand the culture of the West, one must try to understand its behavior toward the Other, toward its possible alternatives which it places in question. Seen from this perspective, the "history of sexuality" continues what was begun in the "history of insanity."

In his obituary on George Bataille (1963) entitled "Preface on Transgression" the theme of sexuality surpasses for the first time the topics of insanity and dreams. Following Bataille's mystery of "holy Eros," Foucault maintains that today only sexuality is capable of filling the emptiness that is encompassed by death and finitude into which the human being was "thrown" as a consequence of God's death. At the same time, it makes possible a "transgression" or crossing of the boundary to the Other. However, instead of language becoming erotic, the opposite has occurred, whereby sexuality has

since the time of Sade and the death of God been thrown into
a universe of language and has been consequently denaturalized
by it.[39]

For the first time there is a reference to Foucault's later topic
dealing with the "discursive processing" of sexuality. Now sexuality is no longer the One, but rather the Other of the discursive
order of our culture which can be understood only when one tries
to understand its behavior towards its opposite Other.

From a totally different perspective, Foucault's structuralistic-
positive turn leads to a similar result. The disinterested, outward
observer of an event perceives only the external side of things.
Consequently, the human being as an "object" becomes a body.
Its most elementary expression outside of those connected with
the preservation instincts of hunger and thirst is sexuality. And
this means for the positivistic-historical theory of power that
power—in the sense of the non-discursive restrictions on the outer
self (i.e. on his body and sexuality)—will be studied.

Concerning finally the power-knowledge complex, it can be
demonstrated that sexuality has always been subjugated to the
power practices of "discourse." At this point there occurs a complete turnaround. Sexuality is not the Other of discursive power.
It is not its target or its object, but rather its quintessence or subject. As a mechanism it entails the disciplining of an individual
body which controllingly unites it with an entire population; sexuality also contains the discursive processing of an individual consciousness upon which it imposes a permanent need for confessing guilt. The old concept of sovereign power was based on the
possession of property and accumulated wealth. The target of the
modern sexual *mechanism* is based conversely on the body and
its energies which in the course of time have become the work
forces and motor for the expansion of capitalistic productivity.[40]
Sexuality, the former Other, has now revealed itself as the integrating principle of the Same. An opposing Other is now hardly recognizable within the context of the Dionysian world of desire
or insanity. What now?

I maintain that the question here concerns only an apparent contradiction. Foucault maintains that the One is based on the silence of the Other. In truth, he never abandoned his earlier Nietzschean dualism; there exists occasionally the aspiring world of Dionysian desire and frequently the Apollonian world of discursive differentiation which it is necessary to combat provided that it is only this and nothing else. In *The Order of Discourses* the division still corresponds on the one hand to the uniqueness and materiality of discourse and on the other to the repressive controls of discourse. Concerning the change to the apparent monism of power, a decisive question remains unanswered: if power fulfills itself as the process that effects discourse, subjectivism and individuality, which of the pre-discursive, pre-subjective and pre-individual will be discoursed, subjected and individualized? One may also ask, from where will come resistance to the total power of discipline, to the sexual *mechanism* and to bio-power. Foucault's answer: "The basis for the counterattack (is) not sexual desire, but rather the body and pleasure."[41] Sexual desire is part of the sexual *mechanism*, while the body and pleasure as may now be inferred represent its external side. They are consequently that which is to be discoursed, subjected and individualized; consequently there arises the battle cry of "denaturalized." The pre-discursive, anarchistic world of the "body and pleasure" is the silent prerequisite for the apparent monism of "discursive" power. For nowhere is it explained to us what the meaning of "the body and pleasure" is if it is not desire, sex or sexuality. The total Other exists nevertheless. This means then that *The Will to Knowledge*, contrary to its conscious target, has basically remained the repressive theory. The discursive world of power suppresses the pre-discursive, anarchistic world of "the body and pleasure." The dualism of the battle cry has remained the abstract basis for the later power theory. Despite its important, convincing and detailed insights, Foucault's power theory failed.

This has remained practically unnoticed. The fascination that his power theory has stirred in many people has been very great.

We know exactly what we are up against, namely practically everything, against the whole social world. At the same time one privately has at one's disposal an indefinite point of retreat: the unimagined world of anarchistic and pleasurable surrealism. This appears to me to be another nerve of the present age that Foucault unintentionally hit.

Madness and Civilization appears thereby in a new light. The fundamental dualism of this early work is the basis of Foucault's entire work up to at least the year 1976. If he reported toward the end that the entire outline of his work was already contained "in a perhaps confused manner" in *Madness and Civilization*, then he was apparently so unconscious of the real confusion that this book fundamentally made that he was unable to solve it despite many great attempts. Foucault's entire work may now be reinterpreted, especially his two most important and material writings, *Madness and Civilization* and *The Order of Things*. The break resulting from the transition can be omitted because it basically did not occur. Self-criticism as a process of inversion did not succeed in freeing itself from the premises that were open to criticism. The tragic dualism in Nietzsche's early work had continually overtaken all attempts to flee from it. Consequently, May of 1968 did not end, at least not in 1976.

CHAPTER

4

RELATIONSHIPS TO THE SELF

THE USE OF PLEASURE AND *THE CARE OF THE SELF* (1984)

The continuation of the series *The History of Sexuality* begins with a dual drum-beat: namely, back to antiquity and back to the subject! Foucault had dropped his original project for a history of modern sexuality. He had intended to separate the four figures of the sexual *mechanism*. The original plan was envisioned as Volume 3: *The Children's Crusade* (the child as pedagogical object), as Volume 4: *Population and Races* (the couple and races as object of the social sciences), as Volume 5: *The Woman, the Mother and the Hysteric* (as the object of medicine), and as Volume 6: *The Perverts* (as the object of psychiatry). A book on the early Christian history of sexuality (Volume 2: *The Confessions of the Flesh*) was to precede these essays. Instead Foucault wrote a book on classical Greece during the fourth century BC (*The Use of Pleasure*) as well as a second on Hellenist-Roman late antiquity during the first and second centuries after Christ (*The Care of the Self*). Completed, however, was the fourth volume of *The History of Sexuality*, which bears the title of the former second volume (*The Confessions of the Flesh*) and has as its subject the third and fourth centuries after Christ. It is not clear whether or not this volume ever appeared posthumously.

Foucault goes back not only to antiquity but also to the subject. He introduces now the third shift, the third axis of subjectivity or the "ethical axis," to which the theoretical work of the fourth and last productive phase is dedicated. Now he is interested in the forms, in which the individuals *as subjects* of sexuality can and must be recognized. These forms are in a theoretical and practical sense the object of ethics (in an ambiguous way the object of a theoretical-philosophical discipline and of concrete experience). In place of the earlier discourse and power practices appear now the self-practices, within whose limits antiquity made sexual activity and pleasure problematic by imparting to them the goal of a spectacular "aesthetics of existence." And in place of the "subjects," of the subject-servant, of the totally dependent "subject," which had completely disappeared in the anonymous knowledge and power relationships because it was completely subjected to them, in the anonymous, original free subject was brought forth.

Since 1966 Foucault had substituted the project for the "disintegration of the subject," and yet even in *The Will to Knowledge* one can see in good poststructuralistic terms how the various relationships of power and resistance "destroy entities and foil, crush and transform individuals."[1]

The transition from the third to the fourth phase completed itself not only as a mere "shift" but rather again as a radical break. Now, for the first time in two decades, the discussion centers again on free subjectivity. "Subjectivity" is understood to be the relationship of the self to the self,[2] which is the self's relationship to existence.[3] "Freedom" does not mean now that the subject is no longer subjugated to the determining complex of power and knowledge but rather that it is able according to its own means to react to the manner of its subjugation either by complying or resisting. No longer is the subject so helplessly abandoned to them, as Foucault had appeared to suggest before, but rather it has the space and freedom by which it *can* react to them this way or that way.

The subject (resides) over practices of subjugation or in an autonomous fashion over the practices of liberation and freedom.[4]

This "and" signifies a development. The original ability and means to freedom allow a liberation from the existing, intolerable power relationships whose changing will make possible once and for all real *freedom*. And what does that mean? It means that one *can* live according to one's capabilities to be free as much as one desires.

Foucault's investigation of the practices by means of which individuals "introduce a certain relationship between self and oneself"[5] is a return to the question posed in *Madness and Civilization*, in which the concern is on the archaeology of the psychological "relationships of the self to the self."[6] The difference is that the psychological relationship that was then evaluated negatively now undergoes a positive evaluation as an existential self-relationship. Irrespective of that, the return confirms the original position which I ascribe to Foucault's early work.

Instead of inquiring about the conditions for the disintegration of the subject, Foucault asks now about its sovereign formation, by which it is able autonomously to create from its own life a beautiful work. His ethics are divided into three levels: that of the moral *codes*, which prescribe to individuals how they should live, their actual moral *behavior*, which obeys or resists the code and the *self-practices* by which an individual constitutes him or herself as a moral subject. According to the manner in which the three levels interact with one another, one can speak neither of a code-oriented morality by virtue of which the moral subject "must be subjugated" to prescribed codes, nor of a general moral law stating that "if it fails to do so, [it] will incur punishment."[7] Or one can speak of a "morality oriented to ethics," which conversely permits the individual to apply sovereign self-practices, by which the individual is able to create the possibility for a beautiful life. According to Foucault the first type of morality is Christian, while the second has as its basis the ancient ways of life, which can be historically traced and which Foucault is investigating, thus his recourse to antiquity.[8]

The fact that this break was more radical than any previous one becomes clear in the fourth phase, which practically annuls the poststructuralism of the second and third phases. In place of the multifarious power relationships, in which the subject is "shredded," there now appears the unity, by way of which it is able to live as it wants. Moreover, there occurs with the subject-theoretical turn also a power-theoretical turn. Power is now no longer a monistic principle. It is rather a determinant for social relationships between people, for communication and for practical action.[9] In addition, it is no longer oriented to a power theory, but rather to a theory of action defined as "acting upon actions"[10] as "effects of certain ways of acting."[11] As a structuring principle for possible action power no longer has an "opposite" or counter power, but rather has the freedom to be an active subject whose rebelliousness constantly provokes power and to whose constraints the subject can react in a variety of ways.[12] Apparently Foucault had given up his poststructural attempts to consider power monistically as a comprehensive network of power relationships containing an anonymous subject. There is something more than power, namely, communication and work, and within its direct sphere of influence there is even more than that, namely freedom.

Accordingly there occurs also a shift in the thematic composition of the power theory. In place of discipline and bio-power Foucault is increasingly interested in that which he calls "pastoral power."[13] With this term he implies a form of power that cares for the well-being of the free members in a community according to the model of the Christian shepherd and keeper of souls. According to Foucault the power practices of modern ways to govern go back to the Christian techniques of caring and managing the soul, which as techniques of *gouvernement* attempt to structure the possibilities of action for free individuals.[14] It is clear to the Nietzsche connoisseur that Foucault sides with his master and especially with the third part of *Genealogy of Morals*.[15]

What has happened? What has caused Foucault to again undergo a radical change? Perhaps it is especially due to the fact that his former power theory failed (and now was, of course, being promptly revised). Either it is nothing at all what it claims to be and contradicts itself, because it secretly has remained the dualistic theory of repression that it claimed to combat, or it is in actuality what it claims: a monistic theory for a power *principle*.[16] But then it is has reached an impasse without any exits, since there doesn't appear anymore a way out of the total context of bio-power.[17] The theory of power sits firmly in a cage which it has built for itself and even possible resistance of subjects against power appears as its product or correlation. Foucault wanted especially to uncover and combat the domain and sphere of activity of bio-power because he viewed it as a major danger.[18] Why? Because it functions at the same time as an objective, subjective, all-encompassing and individualistic source. It subjugates the individual bodies to disciplines and whole populations to controls while simultaneously bringing individuals into a relationship with themselves through the "hermeneutic theory of desire" that triggers the practice of compulsory confession. Even that which we consider our most subjective side is the product of discursive power. There is no more escaping. Therefore, there occurs the third and last shift of the axis to subjectivity which confronts the danger that the former power theory itself created.

Which of the two possibilities should we follow for interpreting this shift? I suggest "alternative" routes, from which, I have always maintained, the truth could be found. In other words one can eliminate in this manner self-contradiction and the uncertainty of the "mysterious" and admit that Foucault basically conceived modern power as a negative duality of repression. One can now more exactly determine from where resistance against repression appears. In the end this is what Foucault himself actually did. Power is repression, insofar as it limits or obliterates autonomous action and the freedom of individuals (which according to Foucault Christian morality had done.)[19] The autonomy of free individuals is then also that which makes possible resistance against such limitations.

Of course power can be the quintessence of a positive non-repressive duality so long as it provides advice, as in antiquity, for how the individual can sovereignly govern his life.

Perhaps we can divide Foucault's life work into different decades:

1. In the 1950s he was especially oriented to Heidegger's philosophy of free subjectivity, where the potential for self-determining a plan of existence was subject to social repressions. This was especially the case when they were "abnormal."[20]

2. In the course of the 1960s he became an archaeologist of knowledge and wrote a "theoretical" philosophy of objective, autonomous and anonymous discourse and knowledge formation.

3. In the 1970s he became an archaeologist for the genealogy of power and adhered to a "practical" philosophy of objective, autonomous and anonymous *mechanism* formation.

4. In the 1980s he finally became an ethical writer who outlined a draft for an existential philosophy of sovereign, individual self-relationships.[21]

It appears that he went from the extreme of an "objective" orientation in the second and third phase to a "subjective" orientation in the last phase. One can look at the course of his theoretical work and its supposedly unconscious logical development as a circle that completes itself and ends where it began, but was enriched as a result of much revised work during the middle phases. From the perspective of the "axis of subjectivity" the asymmetry of the basic relationships in the middle phases can be removed. In these phases the "axis of knowledge" and the "axis of the power practices" form simultaneously the basic axis. Both knowledge and discourse formations and the power practices or mechanism can equally be imagined from the perspective of the subject, that is, according to its reaction to the demands that they place on it. This is the meaning of the triangle which I began with in the Introduction: knowledge-power-subject.

This implies also a return to Heidegger. Indeed Foucault admitted in an interview that Heidegger was for him the "important" philosopher, even when Nietzsche, whose acquaintanceship he owed to Heidegger, was the one who carried the day.[22] In actuality Foucault's existential philosophy of the last phase is descended from Heidegger's *Being and Time*. In this early work Heidegger extensively criticized the entire tradition in modern philosophy of *consciousness* and of the *subject* because from them one could not view subjectivity as a purely internal relationship "of the self to itself," but rather conceived of it as "being." By this Heidegger means a relationship of the self to one's own temporal existence which is always present in the world, that is, within the total context of situations involving actions.[23] We immediately recognize something: Foucault's criticism of the purely self-relationship (regardless of whether or not it is of psychological or Christian origin) is that, as a structure for the "human being," it ought to be removed along with its practices, which the discourse genealogically traces back to social and cultural practices.

The "return to Heidegger" does not contradict Nietzsche's final victory. One can also finally speak of a "return to Nietzsche *through* Heidegger." Perhaps Foucault had in the end only inverted the principle of power that was influenced by Nietzsche and had dominated his entire work. Perhaps the existential ideal of the last phase is an inversion of an objective, autonomous and anonymous power to a power which now is associated with the self-authority of the sovereign individual philosopher who fashions his own life despite all obstacles. Heidegger meant something similar with "real" existence.[24] Nietzsche's polemic contrast of the ancient "master morality" associated with creative-sovereign individuality and the Christian "herd morality" associated with the universal, general, divine laws that are subordinate to human equality[25] shines through in Foucault's comparison of ancient and Christian morality. It will now be shown that this relationship is not so simple.

With regard to the moral code, the eras of classical Greek

antiquity, the Hellenistic-Roman period of late antiquity and those during the gradual spread of Christianity hardly distinguish themselves from one another. All prescribe equally a regulation of desire, the law of monogamous loyalty, a ban on mutual homosexual desire and a theoretical problematization of unsettling sexuality. These four prescriptions correspond to the four objects of ethical problematization and to the four arts of living associated with them: the body (nutrition), the woman or spouse (economics), the male youth (eroticism) and truth (philosophy). The eras differ in the manner in which the four arts of living and the self-practices associated with them (as unchanging moral prescriptions) are practiced and lived.

In *The Use of Pleasure* Foucault determined that in Greece the four arts of living had, from the fourth century BC, the purpose of giving one the choice of one or the other structure. Moreover, self-control was a necessity that freedom made possible through prudence and moderation. In those days the desires were dark, excessive powers, whose spell one easily succumbed to. Therefore, they became a problem and an object of ethical concern not for any inherent reason, but with respect to their excess or absence and with respect to a given point in time and the manner in which they occurred. The greatest evil was considered to be passivity, the surrendering to desire or being enslaved by it. There existed the shameful equation that consisted of passivity = effeminacy = subjugation. Active moderation and self-control were the highest values. If one could control the pleasures, then one could use them freely and sovereignly and—according to the terms of an "aesthetics of existence"—turn one's life into an exemplary masterpiece.

The aforementioned equation suggests that ethics and politics were closely connected. The person who knows how to practice self-control was legitimately entitled to rule over others like him- or herself, women, children and slaves. The ancient ethics was a master morality. Its immediate addressees were only a few—the power elite of free men.

The means that the rulers employed to gain victory over themselves and others was reason. Reason determined the degree of nutrition, physical comforts related to eating and drinking, work for one's own body and ascetic practices. Rulers regulated the economy and demanded from both marital partners a concern for healthy offspring; they regulated the asymmetrical rights and duties for masters and servants, that is, for women, children and slaves.

If these particular arts of living appeared relatively unproblematic, then the third art of living—related to eroticism— became a burning and unsolvable issue. In a patriarchal society— which consistently viewed "masculine" dominance, activity and penetration as its highest values—the equal objectives of pleasure and the honorable concern for the free man were consequently only for those of one's own kind, that is, free men. The consistency of this code of honor contains, however, a contradiction: at least one of the two lovers is obliged to play the passive and subordinate role. As a result of this contradiction there arose the fourth most radical art of living, which was the theoretical problematization of pleasure in the form of a philosophy.

Above all pederasty became a serviceable and shrewd solution to the contradiction. Boys were indeed men but not completely. It was, however, in the final analysis, not so simple because a second patriarchal problem was soon apparent. Because boys were not completely men, but would some day *become* men, they did not have to unconditionally accept their humiliating role as preferred and passive objects of pleasure. Consequently, the adult male lover was required to render pedagogical rewards in return for what was taken away from the boys as a result of the erotic practices; namely an education leading to respectable manhood under the pedagogical wings of Eros. By such means it became possible to transform a humiliating sexual partnership into a valuable friendship.

Foucault's ingenious analysis[26] completes at this point an accomplishment that I had inquired about in the Introduction. It succeeded in connecting genealogy and archaeology at the level of ethical problematization and indeed at a level that cannot be imagined as any more basic. From the lowest layer of "logical" problematization, Foucault the archaeologist unearths his own discipline: philosophy. Archaeology can release its most basic forms of knowledge after genealogy has shown how the forms of knowledge proceed from those very problematic practices. The holder of the professorial chair for "the history of cognitive systems" at the Collége de France has arrived at his topic: sexuality and truth. Is philosophy then a fictitious solution to a social-structural problem in a patriarchal society?

Plato's *Symposium* completed the described path. The question concerning the delicate status of the beloved became the question of love "as such" according to its "ideal essence" or according to what it was believed to be "in truth." Pederasty purified itself by becoming a love of wisdom, by becoming a philosophy. The difficulties in a problematic use of pleasure appeared solved. The repulsive relationship was inverted and turned inside out. In place of pederasty appeared the love of the boy for the wisdom of the teacher (as with Socrates). The lover was now the passive boy and the beloved became the active philosopher, educator and giver of knowledge. Sexual dominance was replaced by the gentle rule of a philosophy that recommended abstinence from physical-sexual activity in order to release the intellectual powers of the human "bcing" of men. Philosophy is a purifying exercise from physical-material turbidity, an ascetic art of life. Let us remember that Foucault himself adhered to this foregone conclusion about philosophy and even demanded it.

The Care of the Self shows that in the first and second century after Christ there appeared an intensification of sexual morality on all levels. The act of sex becamc more and more pathological and permitted only in the context of marriage. Heterosexual love became subject to the demands of symmetrical mutuality and pederasty became increasingly forbidden. In place of the moderate enjoyment of pleasures there appeared in growing degrees—as reflected especially in Stoic philosophy—the *care* of the self, which appeared more and more as a pressure to control oneself. Pleasures then appeared as threatening to the arts of living instead of fulfilling them.

Moreover, the connection between ethics and politics, between mastery over the self and over others, loosened. Although it exclusively serves to a greater degree the creation of the sovereign individual and to a lesser degree a political end, self-mastery appears more and more as an end in itself. Super-individual concerns are no longer the specific point of interest of the city-state, but rather are general and serve to unite all rational beings. One should practice self-control not because it serves a political command, but rather because one is a rational being.

Foucault's correction of the Nietzschean assumption that Christianity inverted the master values of ancient ethics is obvious. Both eras are linked with the continuity of unchangeable rules. Ancient ethics specifically paved the way for Christian ethics, from Platonic asceticism and the demand for abstinence and symmetrical reciprocity in sexual relations as well as from stoic acceptance of direct participation in the world of reason.

Nevertheless, the self-practices in classical antiquity as well as in late antiquity are far away from Christian sexual morality. Foucault moves somewhat again in Nietzsche's direction. Even in late antiquity the suppression of sexuality is not a concern. Even if the use of desire became a more delicate affair, desire was recognized then and before as natural. Christianity, on the other hand, viewed it as a sin. Moreover, Christian morality demanded from everyone submission to divine law. By comparison, ancient ethics formulated sensible rules which were suggested to the individual as a possible means to attain the good life. If Christianity proclaimed "feminine" values such as virginity, physical intactness, purity and passivity, then ancient sexual morality was based upon the "masculine" values of active sovereignty and mastery. Confronting its asymmetry was the Christian demand for symmetrical reciprocity and equality, a demand that addressed everyone while ancient morality was aimed at only a small, elite group of free men. If the concern here was with a pleasurable unity of sexual experiences, then Christian sexual morality separated desire from action and action from pleasure. The Christian technique of "self-decoding" confronted the ancient ascetic techniques; it demanded a hermeneutics of desire which was supposed to anticipate the exercise of sinful sexual acts; and if they were necessary, then this was not for the sake of pleasure, but rather for procreation. Consequently there developed a new relationship of the subject to itself whose boundaries of self-abandonment were easily crossed. Opposing the pure inner relationship of the self was a self-relationship that ancient ethics was aiming for, whereby the self existed in relation to its own existence and to its inner and external condition. The "self" should first of all develop itself, while in Christianity the self was considered a given that had to be probed and "purified."

With this the circle was closed. Foucault had found a connection to the thematic contents in *The Will to Knowledge* and to the analysis of the medieval practices of confession and of those restraints that employed and incorporated these practices. The continual "dissolution of the subject" is now a historical process whose critique presupposes a theory of intact and undamaged subjectivity. In the end Foucault has gone behind his former poststructuralism to an "existential" structuralism. In place of dissolution, of going beyond the self, of the disappearance and dissipation of the subject, there appears in his work a unified structure of existence that is the concern of the "self-practices." The attention of the historian of ancient sexuality was directed to this structure, which he finally developed. I was speaking here within the context of an existential ideal of individual self-determination, which Foucault adopted from Nietzsche and Heidegger and which probably led him to the idealization of historical reality.[27] For the sake of this existential aspect, he probably ignored other aspects of ancient sexual morality, for example, its connection to the repressive effects of certain political powers. Conventional ancient ethics was based upon a competitive and completely code-oriented value system that influenced horrific internal and external sanctions such as shame and disgrace.[28] It is astonishing that Foucault, the theoretician of power, had cut out these associations.[29] But which historian would not choose to do so?

ETHICS AND POLITICS

From the previous chapter it seems that Foucault was able to find in the end a delicate balance between the extremes of his diverse developments. In the context of his symmetrical knowledge-power-subject triangle, the difficulties of the earlier phases seemed to be superfluous. If one, however, considers this development from the perspective of its political consequences, then the question arises about its possible collapse into two irreconcilable extremes of a subjectless-objective power theory and a subjective ethics. The first extreme would be totally political. Power is everything and power is war, reiterates Foucault. To the inversion of the famous formula by Clausewitz, Foucault adds: Politics is a continuation of war with other means.[30] It is accordingly a permanent confrontation of strategic powers that occurs everywhere, a complete policy oriented to action.[31] Instead of speaking of total politics, one could speak of a politics without ethics that is without any normative orientation.[32] The other extreme would be ethics without politics and the private retreat to an art of living whereby the individual becomes a law unto himself.[33]

Both extremes can, however, be nothing more than opposite sides of the same coin. Politics oriented to change and action that has no standards or values is egotistical and selective. It appears to lack a moral orientation and higher political standards that serve the common good.

Upon closer observation, it is obvious that Foucault had never given up the theoretical and especially political perspectives of *Madness and Civilization*. Basically he always combated the sociocultural order of egalitarian "normalization," that strove to rid the world of the irregular Other (who was represented by the insane, the sick, the delinquents, the perverted and "the body and pleasures.") These types were not of a character that could be expressed in a permissible and acceptable language. From the other perspective the homosexual Michel Foucault wrote an ethnology of his own culture that tallied the political consequences for decisive partisanship with Others—those excluded and discriminated against. Foucault was exactly that which was said of him by his rival Sartre,

> a philosopher in the most modern sense of the word, since he essentially reduces philosophy to a form of political activity.[34]

Whether Sartre and Foucault have reduced philosophy to political activity remains to be seen (if it is not decidedly in doubt). In any case, the two philosophical rivals[35] did not have the least problem in participating in political actions, protests or other rallies of solidarity.

The best testimony of Foucault's political orientation is the essay *The Life of Infamous People* (1977).[36] The "infamous people" whom Foucault is interested in are not the glorious heros or the sly bootlickers of power, but rather the small people, the insignificant, unhappy or miserable existences, which are offensive, bothersome or non-conforming. They are the nameless and forgotten whom we no longer know anything about. They are the ones who have been, for a long time, in a disadvantageous position with respect to power.[37] Prison records, police reports and the archives of power are the only monuments that history has granted them. That is the perspective that Foucault takes with respect to his major theme—power. Beneath the memory of power the lives of the infamous people have been irretrievably lost. Foucault's history of power is the history of the lost.

Perhaps some readers have been reminded of Walter Benjamin, who had a similar view of society.[38] The diagnosis of *Madness and Civilization*, which has spread in western culture in the form of a rational system that tended to suppress in a barbaric fashion the Other, shows, moreover, a similarity with the "critical theory" of Herbert Marcuse, Max Horkheimer and Theodor W. Adorno. Foucault became conscious of the similarities only later.[39] Just as the "critical theory" prepared the way for the German (and American) student revolts, so also did Foucault's [ideas] prepare them in France. He did not know at the time that the criticism in the "critical theory" of the bourgeois-capitalistic society in the 1930s was connected with a criticism of the Stalinistic strangulation of socialism. Foucault saw himself confronted with this fact in the 1950s. The pupil of Althusser, Foucault, had also been for a short time a member of the Communist Party in France. The leftist intellectuals, who were at the time dominated by the Communist Party of France, wanted to know nothing of his social perspectives that warned about the excesses of Stalinism.[40] Only a very few intellectuals like Barthes, Blanchot and the English anti-psychiatrists were interested in his studies.[41] Disappointed, Foucault turned away from politics. That may also have been the reason why the theorizing in the second phase, between 1962 and 1968, turned its back on politics.

Suddenly in 1968 everything changed. All at once Foucault's philosophy was in the middle of a real political debate. The Communist Party increasingly fell into the crossfire of leftist critics. In the 1970s the "Nouveaux Philosophes" (Glucksmann, Lévy, etc.) referred to Foucault as they moved from the left to the right and denounced socialism as barbarism and communism, as the bloodthirsty megalomania of power hungry intellectuals. However, Foucault's criticism was not aimed at theoretical Marxism, but rather at the political practices within the Marxist-Leninist parties.[42] His problem was how a revolutionary practice was possible without a centralized and hierarchical party apparatus, which imposed its decisions from above on the masses to which it proclaimed itself the vanguard. Its consequences recognizably distorted its politics. Complete societies were confined and locked in and monitored by the Stalinistic secret police. A revolution of the means of production would not, according to Foucault, change anything for the better unless the power relationships had been revolutionized. The real question is whether a revolution today is at all desirable.[43] Foucault's political considerations had been affected by the crisis within socialism.

His theory of modern power relationships does not, however, suggest that one should expect a lot from the bourgeoisie or social-democratic reform parties or from state organizations in western societies. It was their development against which Foucault chiefly directed his power theory. The idea of political representation disguises the actual power relationships and the practice of representation has welded together the class of politicians with the socially and economically powerful groups in society. Both have long ago separated themselves from any real connection to those they represent,[44] not to mention those discriminated against and excluded from our society. If any person should be in the position to explode the foundation of the existing power relationships in order to change them, then Foucault hopes that person does not become corrupted by the existing controlling powers.

The crises of socialism and of liberal parties with a western orientation reveal only a third practicable path: anarchy (also called "spontaneity" in 1968), which historically has been rejected by rulers because it denounces any form of dominance. This solution wants all to participate in and become part of social movements and local revolts involving, for example, anti-psychiatry, school and university students, homosexuals,[45] women,[46] the disabled and the imprisoned. In 1970 Foucault initiated a survey among prisoners who gave him information on prison conditions. At the time of the prison revolts in 1971 Foucault founded, together with other leftist intellectuals, the G.I.P. (the Group for Prison Information).[47] His collaboration in the G.I.S. (the Group for Health Information) followed.[48] Foucault participated in many isolated actions and political protests regarding, for example, political trials, police repression, racial unrest and political suppression in other countries as in the case of Klaus Croissant, the former *RAF* (Red Army Faction) attorney, whose deportation from the Federal Republic of Germany was to be prevented, or in the case of Peter Bruckner, who was threatened with a ban to practice his profession because he was reproached for having conspired with the *RAF*. These are only two examples that involved the Federal Republic of Germany. Foucault drew attention to the political circumstances surrounding crime and punishment and sued the existing superstructure of the government for the rights (along with human rights and the rights of the citizen) of the governed. He was equally distant from the usual fictitious battles between the cheap "aloofness" of the "public enemies" and their self-righteous condemnation on the one side and the uncritical identification with them on the other.

Discipline and Punish came from the experiences he acquired from the prisons. The experiences made him aware of the weaknesses in the traditional power theories. Power is not merely repression, but rather a productive disciplining and transformation of the body. With time the political dimension of his political theory took shape. If the existing power relationships are more or less the political superstructure of a basic network of decentralized, local and physical confrontations, then one must combat the power centers at their level and on their terms. The goal of political resistance is the subversion of the "macro-physics" of power at the level of "micro-physics" in local confrontations.[49] Foucault's maxim is that one should throw sand into the gears. This is effective in all situations, private and public, at school and at the work place, inside and outside of institutions, in short, any place where one suddenly finds oneself—power has no center. It is a decentralized, omnipotent network of isolated power relationships. The classical form of resistance of the centrally guided political struggle, the representative demonstration, the strike or even revolution, must be replaced with a type of individual protest and dissonance.[50] This will emancipate the inner correlation of power, the single, non-representative form of resistance. The prototype of this dissident is the "infamous person," the one who is discriminated against and excluded, who rises out of the dark dregs of society and confronts power.[51] He constitutes the resistance of the plebeian and commoner.

What role does the intellectual play? He fights with the means of a "politics of truth."[52] Power functions uninhibited only where it can exercise its non-discursive practices in secret and its discursive practices incomprehensibly. It is the task of the intellectual to reflect and reveal the hidden and that which is not understood. The new type of the "specific" intellectual enters into a temporary alliance with the insurgents and provides them with specific knowledge that is befitting to the circumstances in local conflicts. These intellectuals are themselves involved in the conflicts and are affected by them. They don't speak for others, but rather prepare practical information and observe whether the information is useful. In this manner they distinguish themselves from the older type of "universal" intellectual, who dispenses superior knowledge in order to guide the oppressed to freedom. This latter type always knows *from the start* exactly what needs to be done.[53]

In the meantime Foucault, the archaeologist, who formerly was disappointed by and kept a distance from reality, has become the militant genealogist who understands his discipline as a political "discourse battle."[54] However, what is he getting at? What are his positive goals? What are the concrete alternatives to what now exists?

At first his answer is consistent: there are none. Let us consult for the last time the interview with Paolo Caruso from 1969, in which he had portrayed his poststructural philosophical program as the disintegration of the subject, an end to the notion of history as a progressive continuum, and disintegration of illusions whereby actual meaning is a structural image of social reality. If one takes the last one seriously, then the answer to the question concerning the meaning of the political battle can only be *that there is no meaning.* The politics I spoke of at the beginning of the chapter are nihilistic because they are completely without ethics. In the same interview, the information that Foucault gives is curious and functional. Only that type of politics is good that allows society, in the private and public spheres, to operate without friction.[55] Then in 1972 nihilism appears undisguised on the scene. The political battle is an end in itself. According to Nietzsche it serves "great soundness and health," and intensifies one's own power and dismantles "expired power structures."[56] Humane values and ideals of justice do not exist anywhere. Foucault had continually varied this answer until 1984. He is concerned with liquefying solid structures of power[57] and of making a breakthrough by enhancing the multiplicity and diverse individuality of existing power. The impact and political direction of the battle will become apparent only in the battle itself. Who would ever prepare an ethical-political theory and apply it then in a political contest?

Considering the political atmosphere at the time, the radical leftist politics fell between two poles—especially between orthodox communism and social democratic reform. Foucault then raised the question: what can the non-Marxist political left orient itself toward? His answer at the end of the 1960s involved an anarchistic cultural revolution whose power source was Nietzsche's philosophy. Its proclamation of active nihilism is the historical model for Foucault's answer to the question regarding the meaning of the political battle.

If Foucault's entire development was characterized by extreme tension, then the most extreme segment could be found in his political and existential reflections. Typically he found himself (in this case) taking the strongest opposition to his master, Nietzsche. Nietzsche's proclamation of active nihilism was an expression of an aristocratic, anti-plebeian master morality that despised the people as the "herd". Naturally the concept of the "herd" alludes to the Christian designation for the community. To my knowledge, the model for Foucault's support of the small "infamous" people and for the "plebeian" resistance can be found in ethics, that is, in the earliest and most primitive forms of Christianity and its continual periodic and powerless return through the history of Christianity (one may think here of Gioacchino da Fiore, Francis of Assisi or Thomas Münzer). "What you have done to the least of my brothers, you have also done to me."(Matthew, 25,40)[58] According to Marx, "all conditions can be overturned in which the human being finds him- or herself as a humiliated, enslaved, abandoned and despised creature."[59] Giving all power to the absolutely powerless for the purpose of abolishing respective forms of dominance perhaps best formulates the radical democratic ethic of Foucault's anarchism.[60] In actuality he did not totally align himself with the [nihilistic] tradition; he didn't want to and probably couldn't. Nietzsche's attack against Christianity was too strong; on the other hand blood baths were continually committed in the name of the Church, [thereby] discrediting religion. In the final analysis he couldn't align himself with Nietzsche's active nihilism.[61] Why was there so much support for those discriminated against and despised? Why not intensify and fuse one's power with those who already have it anyway?

The extreme tension underlying Foucault's political anarchy is probably due to his opinion characterizing the liberal-democratic "means" as corrupted. All political parties are based on "humanism" just as are established Christian churches. In Christianity's name monstrous crimes have been committed. One may cite here, as an example, the dignity of the civilized Christian, who felt obliged to defend himself against the "wild" brutes, "indians" or cannibals. In the defense of Christian values it is believed that seventy million people have been sacrificed in the history of humanity.[62] For Foucault, the "human being" was a split personality, whose philosophical agony he characterized as "transcendental narcissism." He believed that since the time of Descartes the subject was a synonym for the exclusion of the Other, of an abnormal, ambiguous, peculiar, radically stubborn individualism. The civilized Europeans, in a concentrated action, had hunted down in sixteenth century America their "wild" counterparts.

What are the possible chances for the implementation of anarchistic politics through plebeian resistance? Could it really tackle the superiority of the highly armed state? In 1971 Foucault had hoped for the effective and successful connection between plebeian resistance and the class struggle which was growing in intensity.[63] However, the more he developed his theory of autonomous power, the more totalitarian and inescapable the power structure appeared. From the perspective of mere counterpower, resistance to existing superiority is extremely inferior. In the final analysis it must appear senseless to try to escape from the disciplinary and normalization controls and from the mechanism of sexuality and bio-power. Even in choosing the concept of dissidence there is a revealing side. Normally one uses it to designate resistance to totalitarian regimes. It signifies a political deficiency that is necessitated by the impossibility of organizing a collective and open resistance. As in the former "critical theory" Foucault seems, with his diagnosis of the total power relationships, to have maneuvered himself into an inability to act.

If Foucault placed hope in the effectiveness of social movements, then what was his relationship to the anti-nuclear movement, the peace movement and the ecological movement? How did he evaluate the goals they had been advocating for a long time? If these movements hadn't played for a period such an important role in his own country, one could criticize Foucault's obvious disinterest in them based on his French provincialism. One can also argue that Foucault did not see the major danger in the visible and obvious destructive powers against which these movements had been fighting, but rather only the invisible productive energies of bio-power, which lie closely within us. The more difficult it is to see through its subjective, objective, individual and totalitarian effects, the more dangerous it becomes. The discursive power practices of universal normalization, which discipline the body and our consciousness, continue to impress that which we deem the most inner part of our personality. If this is an unqualified statement then there is no more escape especially since the "Other," the "body and the pleasures," have disappeared in the theory of the unthought of subconscious from *The Will to Knowledge.*

It was also not a secret to Foucault that the "negativism"[64] in battle tactics such as subversion, sabotage, dissidence, plebeian resistance and the liquefying of obstinate power relationships were too little.[65] Repeating what was said before: what is the positive alternative for whose sake one enters a political battle? Foucault's ethical switch placed an answer on the horizon. There is something that is not totally subject to power: the autonomous subject that possesses in the face of power the space for freedom and action. In its name, the ethical tendency should make possible a meaningful and functioning politics.

Perhaps Jean Baudrillard was not completely wrong when he called Foucault's negative politics an "aesthetics of death."[66] In an inverted formulation Foucault issued a more recent answer: the positive alternative is the ethical-political potential for an aesthetics of life or existence.[67] Ethics must formulate what politics can make possible in society, namely rules that are shared by the community that allow the individual without exception to determine by his or her own means a life that is pleasurable and satisfying. Even in the face of social and political relationships, ethics is relatively autonomous.[68]

Consequently Foucault had worn out his former anarchistic anthropology. He no longer imagines the human being as a creature that can dissolve the permanently structured parameters of his or her identity, go beyond the self and multiply the self, but rather conversely as one who is able to (and should) give his existence a strong, unified structure. Politics must now consistently guarantee a social order that makes possible the general application of ethical rules. Near death and existentially confronted with the main theme of his philosophy in the 1960s, which dealt with the finite nature of existence, the seriously ill Foucault probably experienced that his previous anthropology and politics were not livable.[69] The fact that he never expressed himself

on this matter is connected again to his ethically motivated dis-
inclination to feature himself publicly.[70]

Does this turn reveal political resignation? My opinion is that
it does not because Foucault never once departed from the political arena. What he (and many others) had to abandon were the
earlier revolutionary hopes. In place of revolution appeared reform. Foucault worked together on the reform attempts of the
socialist party and union. He actively participated in the debates
on the criminal sexual laws and concerned himself with the social-
political problems of the union movement. He committed himself to Soviet dissidents and to the Polish Solidarity Movement.
He experienced on the spot the Iranian Revolution but later had
to bury the hopes that he had placed in it as mere illusion. And
last, but not least, he devised in his support for the homosexual
movement an outline for a politics of active participation and social safety that would allow, along the lines already mentioned,
an alternative lifestyle—as one calls it today—that would avoid
the two extremes of exclusion and the necessity to conform.[71]

In *The Order of Things* we saw that Kant—alongside Nietzsche
and Heidegger—played an important role in Foucault's philosophy.
Foucault did not, at any time, confuse the modern rationality of
the good "postmodern" (which he had sharply criticized) with the
entire Enlightenment. To this movement belong such figures as
Denis Diderot, whom one can characterize as Foucault's precur-
sor. Like Horkheimer and Adorno, Foucault distinguished between
an unabridged and reduced form of instrumental reason.[72] In the
end he oftentimes referred to Kant's essay *Was ist Aufklärung?*[73]
Kant's outline for an ontology of the present is exemplary in
philosophy when it questions what it means today to be a responsible human being. Already in 1977 Foucault had dreamed of the
intellectual as

the destroyer of evidence and universals, who in unsuspecting mo-
ments and in the duress of the present made recognizable weaknesses, openings and power lines; who constantly changed his po-

sition because he did not know what he would be thinking tomorrow since his attention was always directly solely to the present; who, wherever he may be, contributed his part to the question if the revolution is worth the effort... whereby it is quite obvious that only those could answer this who are willing to put their lives on the line by participating in it.[74]

Both extremes of the subjectless-objective power theory and of subjective ethics, which I outlined at the beginning of the chapter, have proven alongside the corresponding opinions by interpreters of Foucault to be an oversubscription of Foucault's position. His philosophical development took place over the abyss of various intellectual and political divisions. The possibilities for spanning the abyss are purely a matter of perspective.[75] This does not say anything contrary to the equally dangerous and endangered work of a philosopher who constantly put himself and his thoughts and actions on the line. It means simply one thing for us: we will be struggling theoretically and practically for a long time to come with the difficult philosophical heritage this great and troublesome thinker has bequeathed us.

NOTES

Introduction

1. M. Clark, Michel Foucault. *An Annotated Bibliography. Tool Kit for a New Age* (New York, 1983).
2. WzW, p.27. Abbreviations will be used to refer to Foucault's own works. See reference table following the notes.
3. Ibid, p.48.
4. J. Habermas, *Diskurs der Moderne (Discourses of Modernity)*, (Frankfurt, 1974), p.296.
5. AdW, p.30.
6. Ibid.
7. S. Freud, *Totem und Tabu in Studienausgabe*, vol. 9 (Frankfurt, 1974), p.378.
8. GdL, p.15.
9. For other discussions on aspects of post-modernism see the works of J. Lacan and J. Derrida.
10. OdD, p.412.
11. See G. Deleuz, *Foucault* (Frankfurt, 1987), and L. Ferry and A. Renault, *Antihumanistische Denken. Gegen dir Französischen Meister-philosophen* (Munich, 1987).
12. GdL, p.10.
13. Ibid, p.11. See also Chapter 2.
14. Ibid. See also Chapter 3.
15. Ibid, p.10.
16. Ibid, p.12.
17. GE, p.275.
18. GdL, p.12.
19. GE, p.275.

20. GdL, p.12.
21. GE, p.275.
22. GdL, p.19.
23. Ibid.
24. Ibid.
25. GE, p.268.
26. See H.L. Dreyfus/P. Rabinow, *Michel Foucault. Jenseits von Strukturalisimus und Hermeneutik* (Frankfurt, 1987), p.295.
27. SdW, p.24.

Chapter 1

1. The title of the work *Maladie mentale et psycholgie* (1962) is translated into German as: *Psychologie und Geisteskrankheit.*
2. Introduction to the French translation of Ludwig Binswanger's "Traum und Existenz" in Binswanger's "Le rêve et l'existence" (Paris, 1954).
3. In 1946 he began his studies at the Ecole normale supérieure and studied with Althauser.
4. This change is particularly clear in *Maladie mentale et psychologie*, the second volume of *Maladie mentale et personnalité.*
5. See Burger und Irre, "Studie von Klaus Dörner" (Frankfurt, 1969).
6. WuG, p.46.
7. Foucault's interpretation of Decartes was criticized by Jacque Derrida in "Cogito und Geschichte des Wahnsinn," in *Die Schrift und die Differnz* (Frankfurt, 1972).
8. WuG, p.8.
9. Ibid, p.7.
10. Ibid, p.11.
11. Ibid, p.536; WuG, p.386, 549.
12. PuG, p.116.
13. WuG, p.11.
14. Ibid, p.10.
15. F. Nietzsche, *Dir Geburt der Tragödie oder Griechentum und Pessimismus*, in Werke I, ed. by K. Schlechta (Frankfurt, 1976), p.9.
16. WzW, p.74.
17. See works such as R. D. Laing, *The Self and Others*; D. Cooper, *Psychiatry and Anti-Psychiatry*; Also F. Basaglia, ed., *Was ist Psychiatrie?* (Frankfurt, 1974); Basaglia, Foucault, et al., *Befriedungsverbrechen. Über die Dienstbarkeit der Intellektuellen* (Frankfurt, 1980); Cooper and Foucault, *Der eingekreiste Wahnsinn* (Frankfurt, 1979).

18. GE, p.268.
19. WuG, p.15.
20. GdK, p.104.
21. Foucault's structuralist change was under the influence of the positivistic, scientific history of Gaston Bachelard. See Foucault's dissertation, "Le recerce du psychologie," in *Des Chercheurs français s'interrogent* (Toulouse, 1957).
22. See Die Bildung des wissenschaftlichen Geistes (Frankfurt, 1978).
23. Le normale et la pathologique (Paris, 1972).
24. See C. Levi-Strauss, *Strukturale Anthropologie* (Frankfurt, 1972), pp.35, 45.
25. GdK, p.17.
26. AdW, p.284.
27. See M. Frank, *Was ist Neostrukturalismus?* (Frankfurt, 1983), p.197.
28. OdD, p.384.
29. Ibid, p.375.
30. Ibid, p.416.
31. The mathematical and non-mathematical sciences are not treated in depth in Foucault's analysis. More work needs to be done to place Foucalt's Archaeology of the Human Sciences along side Kuhn's Theory of Natural Sciences. See Dreyfus/Rabinow, *Michel Foucault*, loc. cit. pp.102, 229; I. Hacking, "Michel Foucault's Immature Science" in *Nous* 13 (1979); F. Weinert, "Die Arbeit der Geschicte. Ein Verleich der Analysemodelle von Kuhn un Foucault," in *Zeitschrift für allgemeine Wissenschaftstheorie*, XIII, 2 (1982).
32. OdD, p.418.
33. See J. G. Merquior, *Foucault* (London, 1985); Ferry/Renault, *Antihumanistisches Denken*, loc.cit.; J. Améry, "Wider den Stukturalismus. Das Beispiel des Michel Foucault," in *Merkur* 300 (1973); "Neue Philosophie oder alter Nihilismus? Politish-Polemisches über Frankreichs enttäuschte Revolutionäre," in *Literaturmagazin* 9 (Reinbek bei Hamburg, 1978).
34. OdD, p.412.
35. Ibid, p.448.
36. Ibid, p.450.
37. Ibid, p.451.
38. "Neue Folge der Vorlesungen zur Einführung in die Psychoanalsy (New Introductory Lectures on Psychoanalysis)," S. Freud, *Studienausgabe*, Band I (Frankfurt, 1969), p. 496.
39. OdD, p.27.
40. See Levi-Strauss, *Stukturale Anthropologie*, loc. cit., pp,97, 324.

41. OdD, p.458.
42. Ibid, p.365.
43. Kant and the Problem of Metaphysics (Frankfurt, 1951).
44. SdW, p.56.
45. See note 16.
46. See G. Deleuze, *Foucault*, loc. cit., p.135.

Chapter 2

1. Foucault changed the terminology in the second edition of *The Birth of the Clinic* (1972) from that of the first edition (1963). From the perspective of *The Archaeology of Knowledge* he replaced the structuralistic-symbolic terminology with a more discourse analytic one.
2. AdW, p.29.
3. WuG, p.13.
4. AdW, p.71.
5. Ibid, p.29.
6. OdD, p.32.
7. See Foucualt's introduction to *Maurice Blanchot* (Tübingen, 1987), p.14.
8. AdW, p.41.
9. Ibid, pp.100, 234.
10. If I am speaking here of Discourse and Practice, I mean it in the sense of discursive and non-discursive practices.
11. See Foucault, loc. cit., p.25.
12. AdW, pp.224, 233.
13. Because Foucault's Expression theory is unclear and leads to confusion in the *Archaeology*, it is impossible to present a clear discussion here. The reader should refer to other critical works on Foucault.
14. See Foucault, loc. cit., p.69.
15. AdW, p.289.
16. See C. Honegger, "Michel Foucault und die serielle Geschicte," in *Merkur* 407 (1982).
17. AdW, p.292.
18. Ibid, p.182; OdDis, p.48.
19. See C. Kammler, *Michel Foucault. Eine kritische Analyse seines Werks* (Bonn, 1986); M. Foucault, loc. cit., p.17.

Chapter 3

1. See the interview with M. Chapsal in G. Schiwy, *Der Französische Strukturalismus* (Reinbek bei Hamburg, 1969), p.203.
2. SdW, p.24.
3. Ibid, p.9.
4. Ibid, p.8.
5. Ibid, p.14.
6. Ibid, p.9.
7. AdW, p.99.
8. OdDis, p.7.
9. Ibid, p.35.
10. See M. Frank, *Was ist Neostrukturalismus?* (Frankfurt, 1983), p.78.
11. See W. Welsch, *Unsere Postmoderne Moderne* (Weinheim, 1987).
12. SdW, p.83.
13. F. Nietzsche, *The Genealogy of Morals* in Collected Works, vol. 3 (Frankfurt-Berlin-Vienna, 1976), p.235.
14. OdDis, p.7.
15. F. Nietzsche, *The Genealogy of Morals*, p.245.
16. Ibid, p.250.
17. H. Fink-Eitel, "Michel Foucault's Analytik der Macht" in F. A. Kittler (ed.) *Die Austreibung des Geistes aus den Geisteswissenschaften* (Paderborn, 1980), p.38.
18. Üus, p.170.
19. Ibid, p.37.
20. See K. Marx, *Das Kapital*, vol. 1, in Collected Works of Marx and Engels (Berlin, 1971) p.345 and p.349.
21. Üus, p.244; WzW, p.78, 105.
22. M. Perrot, *L'impossbile prison* (Paris, 1980); A. Honneth, *Kritic der Macht* (Frankfurt, 1985), p.187; J. Habermas, *Diskurs der Moderne* (Frankfurt, 1985), p.318.
23. Üus, p.286.
24. WzW, p.34; DdM, p.119.
25. In 1976 Foucault was still positive about Reich's Repression Theory.
26. WzW, p.34.
27. Ibid, p.78.
28. Ibid, p.86.
29. OdDis, p.8.
30. WzW, p.25.
31. Ibid, p.125.
32. Ibid, p.168.

33. Ibid, p.167.
34. Michel Foucault, p.133.
35. See footnote 31 in Chapter 1.
36. *Jenseits von Gut und Böse* in F. Nietzsche, Collected Works, vol 3 (Frankfurt-Berlin-Vienna, 1976), p.33.
37. Ibid, p.47.
38. Ibid, p.72.
39. SdW, p.51.
40. H. Fink-Eitel, "Michel Foucault's Analytik der Macht," p.48 and p.53.
41. WzW, p.187.

Chapter 4

1. WzW, p.118; DdM, p.142.
2. GdL, p.12.
3. GE, p.274.
4. VdF, p.137.
5. GdL, p.12.
6. WuG, p.15.
7. GdL, p.41.
8. See M. Foucault *Genealogie der Ethik*, p.268 in Dreyfus/Rabinow (German Ed.); *Freiheit und Selbstsorge*, p.12.
9. SM, p.251. Here we have the definite influence of Habermas. J. Habermas, *Technik und Wissenschaft als Ideologie* (Frankfurt), p.62.
10. SM, p.255.
11. Ibid, p.254.
12. Ibid.
13. Ibid, p.248.
14. Ibid, p.255.
15. F. Nietzsche, *The Genealogy of Morals*, p.317.
16. Note: Power is for Foucault "a name given to a complete, strategic situation in society."
17. G. Deleuze, *Foucault* (Frankfurt), p.133.
18. GE, p.268.
19. FuS, p.20.
20. A "Heideggerean-Marxist" philosophy appears in the philosophy of Herbert Marcuse. See *Hegels Ontologie und die Grundlegung einer Theorie der Geschichtlikeit* (Frankfurt, 1932).
21. The "Axis of Subjectivity" is at first only a historical analytical framework that Foucault enlarges to an existential philosophy.

22. "La retour de la morale," in *Les Nouvelles littéraires*, June/July 1984.
23. *Sein und Zeit* (Tubingen, 1967), pps.4, 9, 14-18.
24. Ibid, pp.40, 60, 62.
25. F. Nietzsche, *The Geneaology of Morals*.
26. *See J. Boswell, Christianity, Social Tolerance and Homosexuality* (Chicago, 1980).
27. See W. Welsch's review of vol. 1 and 2 of Sexualität und Warheit in *Phil. Lit. Anz.* 39/4 (1986), p.374.
28. See Foucault's own analysis in *Sexualität und Warheit*, pp.247-266.
29. False however is the criticism that Foucault identifies with the ancient pagen-virility ethic. Quite the contrary!
30. ÜuS, p.217; WzW, p.114; DdM, pp.40, 71.
31. See DdM, p.151 and R. Debray, "Auf der Schultern Solschenizyns" in: *Alternative* 116 (October 1977).
32. This fear is shared by M. Frank, *Was ist Neostrukturalismus?*, p.238; J. Habermas, *Der Philosophische Diskurs der Moderne* (Frankfurt, 1985) p.324, and C. Taylor (moderator), *Negative Freiheit* (Frankfurt, 1988), p.230.
33. C. Kammler, *Michel Foucault* (Bonn, 1986), p.203.
34. SdW, p.21.
35. See J. P. Sartre, "Sartre repond" in *Quinzaine littéraire* 14 (1966). See also footnote 1 of Chapter 3.
36. *Tumult* 4 (1982).
37. Foucault had published with Arlette Farge: *Le désordre des familles. Lettres de cachet des Archives de la Bastille* (Paris, 1982).
38. U. Benjamin, *Collected Works*, vol. I.2 (Frankfurt, 1978), p.695.
39. "Ein Gespräch mit G. Raulet" in *Spuren* I (1983); also A. Honneth, *Kritik der Macht* (Frankfurt, 1985), p.196; and "Foucault und Adorno, Zwei Formen einer Kritik der Moderne", in Peter Kemper (Ed.) *Postmoderne oder der Kampf um die Zukunft* (Frankfurt, 1988).
40. DdM, p.23.
41. MdM, p.108.
42. See Fink-Eitel, "Michel Foucault's Analytik der Macht", pp.40, 49, 53; and U. Marti, *Michel Foucault* (Munich, 1988), p.110.
43. DdM, p.193.
44. SdW, p.128; MdM, p.95.
45. See VdF pp.55, 85, 95, 111; and G. Hocquenqhem, *Das homosexuelle Verlangen* (Munich, 1974).
46. See DdM, p.160.
47. MdM, p.5.
48. Ibid, p.80.

49. SdW, p.130.
50. DdM, p.65.
51. Ibid, p.204.
52. Ibid, p.53.
53. SdW, p.128; DdM, pp.44, 227.
54. SdW, p.137.
55. Ibid, p.26.
56. See "Sur la justice populaire," in: *La Temps modernies* 310 (1972).
57. FuS, p.20.
58. See E. Bloch, *Das Prinzip Hoffnung*, vol. 3 (Frankfurt, 1973), p. 148; *Atheismus im Christentum*, (Frankfurt, 1985), p.181.
59. *Zur Kritik der Hegelschen Rechtsphilosphie*, in: Marx-Engels-Werke, vol. 1 (East Berlin, 1957), p. 385.
60. See DdM, p.59.
61. F. Nietzsche, *Werke IV* (Frankfurt-Berlin-Vienna, 1977), pp.142, 149.
62. See T. Todorov, *Die Eroberung Amerikas. Das Problem des Anderen* (Frankfurt, 1985), p.161.
63. J. K. Simion, "A Conversation with M. Foucault," in *Partisan Review* 2 (New York, 1971), p.198.
64. MdM, p.112.
65. See Cooper/Foucault, *Der eingekreiste Walnsinn* (Frankfurt, 1974), p.89.
66. J. Baudrillard, *Oublier Foucault* (Munich, 1978), p.79.
67. GE, p.273; VdF, p.133; "L'éthique de souci de soi comme pratique de liberté," *Concordia* 6 (1984).
68. VdF, p.80.
69. see M. Foucault on Maurice Blanchot, (Tübingen, 1987), p.79.
70. VdF, p.9.
71. J. Rajchman, *The Freedom of Philosophy* (New York, 1985).
72. See "Die Folter, das ist die Vernunft." A conversation between Knut Boesers and Foucault, *Literaturmagazin* 8 (Hamburg, 1977), p.65; M. Perrot, *L'impossible prison* (Paris, 1980), p.31.
73. SM, p.250; VdF, p.123. See also "Q'est-ce que les Lumiéres?" *Magazine littéraire* 207 (1985).
74. DdM, p.198.
75. I hope to shortly produce an essay on Levi-Strauss and Foucault where I will attempt to clarify the problem of the Self.

SELECTED BIBLIOGRAPHY

WORKS IN GERMAN and
LIST OF ABBREVIATIONS

AdW   Archäologie des Wissens (The Archaeology of Knowledge). Frankfurt, 1973 (L'archéologie du savoir, 1969).

DdM   Dispositive der Macht. Über Sexualität, Wissen und Wahrheit. Berlin, 1978.

FuS   Freiheit und Selbstosrge. H. Becker, L. Wolfsteter, A. Gomez-Muller, R. Fornet-Betancourt, eds. An interview from 1984. Frankfurt, 1985.

GdK   Die Geburt der Klinik. Eine Archäologie des ärztlichen Blicks (The Birth of the Clinic: An Archaeology of Medical Perception). Frankfurt-Berlin-Vienna, 1976 (Naissance de la clinique. Une archéologie du regard médical, 1963).

GdL   Sexualität und Wahrheit, Band II: Der Gerbrauch der Lüste (The History of Sexuality. Vol. 2: The Use of Pleasure). Frankfurt, 1986 (Histoire de la sexualité II: L'usage des plaisirs, 1984).

GE   "Genealogie der Ethik (Interview mit Michel Foucault)," in H. L. Dreyfus/P. Rabinow, Michel Foucault. Janseits Strukturalismus und Hermeneutik. Frankfurt, 1987. pp. 265-292.

MdM   Mikrophysik der Macht. Über Strafjustiz, Psychiatrie in Medizin. Berlin, 1976.

OdD   Die Ordnung der Dinge. Eine Archäologie der Humanwissenschaften (The Order of Things: An Archaeology of the Human Sciences). Frankfurt, 1974 (Les mot et les choses. Une archéologie des sciences humaines, 1966).

OdDis   Die Ordnung des Diskurses (Discourse on Language). Munich, 1974 (L'ordre du discours, 1971).

PuG   Psychologie und Geisteskrankheit (Mental Illness and Psychology). Frankfurt, 1977 (Maladie mentale et psychologie, 1962).

SdW   Von der Subversion des Wissen. W. Seitter, ed. Munich, 1974.

SM   "Das Subjekt und die Macht," in H. L. Dreyfus/P. Rabinow, *Michel Foucault. Janseits von Strukturalismus und Hermeneutik*. Frankfurt, 1987. pp. 243-261.

SuS   *Sexualität und Wahrheit, Band III: Dir Sorge um sich* (The History of Sexuality. Vol III: The Care of the Self). Frankfurt, 1986 (Histoire de la sexualité III: Le souci de soi, 1984).

ÜuS   *Überwachen und Strafen. Dir Geburt des Gefängnisses* (Discipline and Punish: The Birth of the Prison). Frankfurt, 1976 (Surveilleur et punir. La naissance de la prison, 1975).

WuG   *Wahnsinn und Gesellschaft. Eine Geschichte des Wahns im zeitalter der Vernunft* (Madness and Civilization: A History of Madness in the Age of Reason). Frankfurt, 1973 (Histoire de la folie a l'âge classique, 1972).

WzW   *Sexualität und Wahrheit, Band I: der Wille zum Wissen* (The History of Sexuality. Vol I: An Introduction. Also known as The Will to Knowledge). Frankfurt, 1977 (Histoire de la sexualité I: La volonté de savoir, 1976).

VdF   *Von der Freundschaft. Michel Foucault im Gespräch*. Berlin, n.d.

WORKS BY FOUCAULT IN ENGLISH

The Archaeology of Knowledge. Trans. by Alan Sheridan. New York, 1972.

The Birth of the Clinic: An Archaeology of Medical Perception. Trans. by A. M. Sheridan-Smith. New York, 1973.

Death and the Labyrinth: The World of Raymond Roussel. Trans. by Charles Raus. New York, 1968.

Discipline and Punish: The Birth of the Prison. Trans. by Alan Sheridan. New York, 1977.

Discourse on Language. Trans. by Robert Swyer. Appendix to The Archaeology of Knowledge.

History of Sexuality. Vol. I: An Introduction (The Will to Knowlegde). Trans. by Robert Hurley. New York, 1978.

History of Sexuality. Vol.II: The Use of Pleasure. Trans. by Robert Hurley. New York, 1984.

History of Sexuality. Vol. III: The Care of the Self. Trans. by Robert Hurley. New York, 1986.

Madness and Civilization: A History of Madness in the Age of Reason. Trans. by Richard Howard. New York, 1965.

Mental Illness and Psychology. Trans. by Alan Sheridan. New York, 1976.

The Order of Things: An Archaeolgoy of the Human Sciences. Trans. by Alan Sheridan. New York, 1973.

SELECTED BOOKS ON FOUCAULT

Arac, J. (ed), *After Foucault: Humanistic Knowledge, Postmodern Challanges*. New Brunswick, 1988.

Bouchard, D. (ed), *Language, Counter-Memory, Practice: Selected Essays and Interviews*. Ithaca, 1977.

Cousins, M. and Hussain, A., *Michel Foucault*. London: MacMillan, 1984.

Dreyfus, A. and Rabinow, P., *Michel Foucault: Structuralism and Hermeneutics*, 2nd edition. Chicago, 1982

Enbon, D., *Michel Foucault*. Trans. by Betsy Wing. Cambridge, 1991.

Gordon, Colin (ed), *Power/Knowledge: Selected Interviews and Other Writings*. New York, 1980.

Kritzman, L. D. (ed), *Politics, Philosophy, Culture: Interviews and Other Writings, 1977-1984*. New York: Routledge, 1988.

Lemert, C. and Gillan, G., *Michel Foucault: Social Theory and Transgression*. New York, 1982.

Merquior, J. G., *Foucault*. Berkeley and Los Angeles, 1985. Sheridan, A., *Michel Foucault: The Will to Truth*. London, 1980.

Smith, B., *Foucault, Marxism and Critique*. London, 1983.

CHRONOLOGY TABLE

1926   Michel Foucault is born on Oct.15 in Paris. His father is a physician.
1945   Primary schooling ends at the Lyceé Henri IV in Paris (one of his teachers is Jean Hippolyte).
1946   Attends the Ecole normale Supérieure in Paris. One of his teachers is Luis Althusser.
1948   Degree in Philosophy.
1949   Degree in Psychology.
1951   "Agrégation" in Philosophy.
1952   Diploma in Psychology, member of the Communist Party in France, assistant at the University in Lille.
1955   Lecturer at the University of Uppsala, Sweden. 1958 Director of the French Center, University of Warsaw. 1959 Director of the French Institute, Hamburg.
1961   Doctorate in Philosophy (with *Madness and Civilization* and a translation of Kant's *Anthropology*).
1962   Professor at the University of Clermont-Ferrand.
1966   Professor at the University of Tunis.
1969   Professorship for the "History of Thinking Systems" at Collége de France in Paris.
1971   Founding of the G.I.P. (Group for Prison Information)
1981   Collaboration with the socialist trade union CFDT.
1983   Sojourn at the University of California at Berkeley.
1984   Michel Foucault dies in Paris.

Hinrich Fink-Eitel (b. 1946) is a lecturer in Philosophy at the Free University in Berlin and at Frankfurt University. His main areas of interest are German Idealism, especially Kant and Hegel, as well as the philosophies of the 20th century (existentialism, Critical Theory, poststructuralism).